How to use our guide

- All the practical information, hints and tips that you will need before and during the trip start on page 102.
- For general background, see the first two sections, Norway and the Norwegians, p. 6, and A Brief History, p. 14.
- All the sights to see are listed between pages 25 and 86. Our own choice of sights most highly recommended is pin-pointed by the Berlitz symbol.
- Entertainment, nightlife and other leisure activities are described between pages 86 and 94, while information on restaurants and cuisine is to be found on pages 94 to 101.
- Finally, there is an index at the back of the book, pp. 127–128.

Although we make every effort to ensure the accuracy of all the information in this book, changes occur incessantly. We cannot therefore take responsibility for facts, prices, addresses and circumstances in general that are constantly subject to alteration. Our guides are updated on a regular basis as we reprint, and we are always grateful to readers who let us know of any errors, changes or serious omissions they come across.

Text: Ken Bernstein
Photography: Walter Imber
Layout: Doris Haldemann
We are particularly grateful to The Oslo Travel Association for their help in the preparation of this book.
Cartography: Falk-Verlag, Hamburg.

4

Contents

Cover picture: School children parading in front of the Royal Palace on Constitution Day

Photo, pp. 2–3: Near Skjolden, Lustrafjord

Norway and the Norwegians

Norwegians take fervent pride in their grandiose scenery. And it's not surprising. Few countries in the world have such vast mountains of eternal snow, valleys of fresh spring flowers, ice-blue lakes and moody green fjords. Here, in this rugged land, you can tell they love the great outdoors. Small wonder that Norwegians invented the world's most popular winter sport: skiing.

At every opportunity, these tall, robust descendants of the Vikings

abandon their tidy towns to take advantage of the nearby seas, rivers or forests. A million Norwegians go fishing; almost everyone skis, even the toddlers. It's a country where businessmen look more comfortable with backpacks than with attaché cases.

Love of nature is matched by love of Norway and there's a national passion for flagwaving and folklore. Every house seems to

Aurora borealis shimmers eerily over cottage in snowy North; colourful flowers completely transform Norway's countryside in springtime.

have a flagpole, every town a museum documenting its ancient or recent past. Elaborately embroidered folk costumes are worn on all special occasions. Perhaps the patriotic gestures are a reaction to the long struggle for Norwegian identity. (After five centuries under foreign kings, independence was not restored until 1905.) On Constitution Day in Oslo, marching bands lead a three-hour parade of school-children past the Royal Palace. The kids carry enough red-white-and-blue Norwegian flags to bedeck every flagpole in Europe. But it's patriotism without a threat to anyone. The parade is a pacifist pageant; it shuns soldiers and guns.

A look at the globe might prompt the question: What's a beautiful country like Norway doing in a place like this? Its geography and topography are downright freakish. About half the country lies north of the Arctic Circle. Oslo is farther north than Yakutat, Alaska, or the end-of-the-line Siberian town of Magadan.

Norway is an impressive 1,088 miles long, yet as narrow as 4 miles at its leanest point. Among European countries, only Iceland has a lower density of population. If the land could be chopped into equal chunks, every one of Norway's four million citizens would be sitting in the middle of nearly 25 acres. But most of them would be out of luck: the country is so hilly and rocky that only 3 per cent of the land is cultivated; and some of that is so steep that even goats have to watch their step.

Wherever you go in Norway—to rocky promontories polished by gales or in claustrophobic arctic valleys which see no sun for two months—the people are plugged in to the life of the nation. Radio and television reach almost every nook and cranny, and at last report only about 300 houses in the whole country were beyond the electricity network. The government aims to build a road, however crude, to every last farm to give every child the chance to get a proper education. (Incidentally, Norway publishes, more books per capita than any other nation— some 2,500 new titles a year. Most are by Norwegian authors although many foreign authors are also popular.)

The electricity which lights and heats even isolated houses is generated by cheap hydroelectric power, so abundant, thanks to the mountain rains and snow, that the surplus is exported to Sweden. The development of this clean "white coal" from the waterfalls has made possible the country's 20th-century transition from relative poverty to the status of an up-to-date industrial power. But beyond this, the recent exploitation of off-shore oil and gas has launched a magic carpet of prosperity. The "blue-eyed Arabs" of Norway, western Europe's first oil-exporting country, have achieved a per-capita gross national product exceeding that of the United States and a standard of living that's the envy of almost all the world.

Not that anyone's showing off the unaccustomed affluence. Most Norwegians are too prudent to be caught in *nouveau-riche* excesses. They still carry a paper bag of sandwiches to the office for a working lunch, roll their own cigarettes and nurse a cup of coffee for an hour in a café. But an ever-increasing percentage of families have acquired those essential Norwegian luxuries—a country holiday cottage and a boat.

Even if ostentation were part of the national character, Norwegians would be unlikely to show off. The tax system—noted for the extraction of huge sums at all levels—is the great equalizer. The revenues pay for the schools and roads (think of the snow removal bill!) and a

Norway—Facts and Figures

Geography:	Area 125,000 sq. miles, plus Arctic and Antarctic possessions. Coastline (including bays, fjords, inlets etc.) 13,110 miles, protected by an estimated 150,000 islands and islets.
Population:	4,000,000, all of Nordic race except about 20,000 Sámi in far north and small influx of foreign workers and refugees.
Government:	Constitutional monarchy: executive power vested in the king and his council, legislative power in the democratically elected *Storting* (parliament).
Industry:	Oil and gas, aluminium, iron and steel, forestry, shipping, fishing.
Religion:	About 95% of the population adhere to the official Church of Norway (Evangelical Lutheran).
Language:	Two mutually comprehensible versions of Norwegian: *bokmål* (influenced by Danish) and *nynorsk* (an artificial compound of Norwegian dialects).

Atlantic's abundance on parade at waterfront fish market in Bergen.

hefty welfare-state cornucopia of pensions, health care and social services. A relatively high proportion of the national wealth goes in overseas aid to developing countries.

Be prepared for a striking side-effect of the economic boom, the high cost of living. This is no place to go for a cheap holiday or bargain shopping. Some things are expensive and other things are *very* expensive. But Norway is mostly a land of pleasant surprises. The climate, for instance, is far more temperate than you might have expected. The Gulf Stream brings a measure of its heart-warming tropical touch all the way to the seas around Norway. And while the mercury has been known to plum-

Best of all, summer brings the Midnight Sun to the northern half of the country. Even down in Oslo and Bergen, in June you can read a book by daylight after 11 p.m. And when the sun finally goes down, it's the gaudiest slow-motion sunset imaginable. The phenomenon of almost limitless sunshine delights the Norwegians even more than the visitors. After the long, dark winter, when they finally feel the warmth of the spring sun, they bask in it as gratefully as deep-sea divers coming up for fresh air.

To mark the summer solstice Norwegians celebrate Midsummer Night. Huge bonfires are lit on hilltops or near the coast, and thoughts turn to the primitive past. Are the fires on the longest day a salute to the sun at its apogee or perhaps a plea for the fertility of the fields? Witches and strange spells can easily be imagined in the brief twilight, just as in the era when the mysteries of the stars ruled daily life. (Miniature witches on broomsticks fly in the windows of souvenir shops, above the inevitable statuettes of doltish, hairy trolls, whittled by far-off farmers on those long winter nights.)

met to – 61°F (–51.4°C) in the Norwegian arctic, the temperature in Bergen only rarely slips below freezing point in darkest winter. The summers are mild with occasional hot spells. Oslo, Bergen and other seaside towns even have bathing beaches and outdoor pools, with the water temperature in the Oslo Fjord actually rising into the 70s°F (20s°C) during the swimming season.

Seeing Norway is more down-to-earth than touring Europe's **11** more sophisticated countries. Norway's towns, mostly small, have modest monuments and few ancient landmarks. Even Oslo, the capital and only sizeable city, is more countryside than cityscape; there are no skyscrapers, but no slums, either. Although it's at the centre of commerce and government, life's not all serious: Did you ever see so many pleasure boats on any town's waterfront? Norway's nautical history fills the museums, too. See Viking boats, the Kon-Tiki raft and other vessels.

Bergen, the second city, remains very much an overgrown fishing village with an atmosphere all its own. Above the steep-roofed medieval harbour district, villas and small wooden houses cluster on the steep green hillsides. The fishmarket and the aquarium here will fascinate you.

But the greatest attraction of all in Norway is the majestic countryside, with thrilling changes of scenery at every turn. If one minute you find yourself in desolate craggy terrain that only an elk

---

Norwegians of Note

Norway has had more than its fair share of the great men of Scandinavia in the realms of culture and discovery.

Ibsen, Henrik. 1828–1906. Dramatist and poet. *Brand, Peer Gynt, A Doll's House, Ghosts, The Wild Duck, The Master Builder.*

Grieg, Edvard H. 1843–1907. Composer, of the nationalistic school. *Piano Concerto, Peer Gynt, In Autumn, Sigurd Jorsalfar, Norwegian Dances, Symphonic Dances.*

Munch, Edvard. 1863–1944. Painter and engraver who had a major influence on the expressionists. *The Sick Child, Frieze of Life, The Scream, Girls on the Bridge.*

Hamsun, Knut. 1859–1952. Novelist. *Hunger, Growth of the Soil, Pan, Under the Autumn Star.* Nobel Prize for Literature.

Nansen, Fridtjof. 1861–1930. Arctic explorer, statesman and scientist. Crossed Greenland (1888–89). Reached the record 86° 14' N with the polar ship *Fram* (1895–96). High Commissioner for Refugees at the League of Nations. Nobel Peace Prize.

Amundsen, Roald. 1872–1928. Explorer and navigator. Discovered the South Pole (1910–11) on the *Fram* ship.

Heyerdahl, Thor. Born 1914. Anthropologist. *Kon-Tiki* and *Ra II* expeditions.

could love, the next you may spy a narrow valley as green as a golf course—and with nicely distributed water traps. As you get closer to nature, you'll feel the harmony of the land: noble mountains accompanied by green lowlands, the mighty force of the sea balanced by placid lakes and burbling rivers. There are more waterfalls than you've ever seen in your whole life—plunging, ricocheting, streaming, wispy… You can follow the whole story from the melting mountain snows cascading into clear, cold lakes, emptying down rushing rivers into the fjords, those incomparably dramatic monuments left by the glaciers of the Ice Age.

You can see the country by car, train, bus, excursion steamer or even by bike. But it's fun to try them all, alternating according to the landscape, the weather, the mood. The way-stations can be as simple as a campsite or country inn, or as luxurious as a grand hotel in one of the towns. Or you can stay at a wilderness holiday hotel built around a heart-stopping

Treasured timbers: only a few of Norway's medieval stave churches survived hazards of the centuries.

view. At most hotels the big bonus is breakfast—a do-it-yourself banquet that can run from pickled herring and salami to cereals and marmalade, with something delicious for every taste.

After that, if you're still up to it, you can join the Norwegians in one of their outdoor pursuits—fishing, boating, water-skiing, golfing, tennis, horseback riding, or just hiking. You can even ski on snow all summer long at certain mountain resorts if the novelty seems irresistible.

After a long day on the road or engaged in healthful sports, you'll probably be too tired for a hectic nightlife—which is just as well, in a country where nightclubs are a rarity and alcohol is punitively priced. In the bigger towns, though, you won't be at a loss in the evening; tourist offices have lists of restaurants, discos, jazz clubs, folk music performances, theatres and concerts.

And, if you're in one of the hamlets where the day's only excitement is the arrival of the mail boat, just relax and let the simple, unaffected life embrace you. Foreign tourists may be a new phenomenon in backwoods Norway, but hospitality has always come naturally.

A Brief History

What a cast of characters! Harald Fairhair, Eric Bloodaxe, Magnus the Good … The saga begun by the Vikings spans 1,000 dramatic years. Yet modern Norway only joined the family of independent nations in the 20th century.

The Vikings were the most celebrated — and notorious — Norwegians. But the land had been inhabited for thousands of years before those intrepid travellers made the world sit up and take notice.

Primitive peoples left clues to the life they led on the peninsula. Hunting and fishing gear, crudely carved from bone and stone, have been found dating from as early as 9,000 or 10,000 B.C. At the time of the late Stone Age, the cavemen of Norway came out to luxuriate in the warm sun as the ice cap receded. They raised cattle and grew grain. Then, glacial weather conditions returned, retarding the arrival of the Iron Age and spreading hard times throughout the northern lands.

Later, in the first and second centuries A.D., thanks to contacts with the Roman empire, Norwegians started to master the technology of iron. They turned it into both swords and ploughshares. Along with primitive industry came the organization of society. Communal lookout posts, refuges and places of pagan worship were established; laws were promulgated. The new communities contained the elements and skills that were later to produce the Vikings with their dragon-prowed longboats and warlike desire for expansion.

The Viking Era

Around A.D. 800 the Norsemen started exploring—and exploiting—the lands across the sea. Many motives have been attributed to these swashbuckling Scandinavian sailors: a lust for power, a search for trade, a need for territory or a thirst for adventure. Some truth can be found in each theory, if only because different expeditions had different goals. Some

---

Odin, Thor, Hel & Co.

For pre-Christian Norwegians, a gallery of gods existed with whom a good relationship was of the utmost importance. To placate them, three main sacrifices (*blot*) took place each year.

The sagas and poetry of old tell the full story of these gods. ODIN, called *Allfader* (Father of All), taught men the art of writing runes and skaldic poetry. Odin not only possessed great wisdom, but was also a fearless warrior—the ideal of the Viking hero figure. And when those who followed him passed into the next world, they were secured a place in his hall where they could go on fighting and drinking mead—forever.

THOR, Odin's son, inherited his father's strength but not his wisdom. The god of thunder, he rode across the sky to fight the other gods, making everything tremble. (Thunder in Norwegian is *torden*.)

FRØY, the god of fertility, was important for the farmers; and HEL was the blackfaced goddess of the realm of death. She awaited all those who died a natural death.

Though the belief in Odin and Thor died away with the introduction of Christianity, the old Norse people still saw the world around them inhabited by trolls. These fantastical creatures lived in the woods, fields, fjords and seas of the Norwegian imagination. Trolls might share one eye (although they often had three heads), and were strong, but stupid. In most of the tales the physically weaker man or boy would overcome the troll with his intelligence.

15

were frankly for private gain—the indelicate word is "piracy". No one denies that pillage and rape were the stock in trade of many early Vikings. But other voyages were designed simply to open new commercial routes, or to colonize new lands.

Three Scandinavian neighbours joined in the epic of Viking conquest. The Swedes, looking east, sent shock waves through Russia and all the way to Arabia. The Danes, physically attached to Europe, concentrated on France and Britain and sallied forth into the Mediterranean. Westward-facing Norway challenged the mysterious, dangerous North Atlantic.

The first Norse expeditions set up bases on the islands off Scotland, moving on to Ireland, the Isle of Man and England. In subsequent forays into France, the Norwegian Viking, Rollo (Gange-Rolv), took control of the whole of Normandy. Later, his descendant William (the Conqueror) went to England to triumph at the Battle of Hastings in 1066.

Ornately carved wagon shares pride of place with three Viking sailing ships preserved in Vikingskipshuset, *museum in Oslo suburb of Bygdøy.*

A more daunting test for Norwegian seamanship led into unknown northern seas, to colonize Iceland and Greenland. At the end of the 10th century, a Viking mission discovered "Vinland" meaning "pastureland". The tale of Leif Eriksson's adventure has often been told and argued. What seems beyond dispute is that Vikings based in Greenland discovered a fertile, inhabited land on the far side of the Atlantic. If the Norsemen's lines of communication hadn't been stretched so thin, they might have established colonies. But at least the Vikings did take a pioneering look at the New World—in Newfoundland (the site was discovered in 1960) and Labrador—about five centuries before Christopher Columbus and Amerigo Vespucci put America on the map.

In places closer to home, where the Vikings planted outposts, ideas were exchanged with the natives, bringing lasting cultural benefits to both sides. The Vikings founded Dublin, Cork and Limerick and taught the Irish how to build and sail seaworthy ships. Elsewhere in their travels, the Norsemen imposed their law and learnt new skills and concepts from those whose territory they had taken. On first meeting Christianity, they plundered the gold and silver of the defenceless churches. But in the end, the beliefs of the plundered rubbed off on the plunderers and they carried the religion back to their homes. By the beginning of the 11th century, Norway was officially a Christian nation.

One Kingdom

A great deal of the knowledge of the next period of Norwegian history comes from the famous sagas of the Norwegian Viking kings composed by Snorre Sturlasson. Of these noble warrior-kings, it was Harald Fairhair who transformed Norway from an agglomeration of warring feudal states into a unified kingdom. A charming legend recounts the story of his conquest, due, it is said, to the love of a woman. Gyda, a beautiful girl, refused his offer of marriage until he had become king of all Norway. Vowing not to cut his hair until he succeeded, Harald fearlessly overcame all rivals on land and sea until he received both crown and Gyda. Those were the days.

King Harald's son, Eric Bloodaxe, proved a less apt statesman and fighter. Though many lives **17** were sacrificed in the effort, Eric failed to control Norway's competing power centres and was eventually driven out of office.

His successor, Håkon I, was educated at the court of King Athelstan in England. He was able to hang on to power and reform the judicial system. Things went so well that the king became known as Håkon the Good. Ahead of his time, Håkon tried to install Christianity as the official religion of Norway, but pagan pressures were so powerful that he failed.

The same task was carried on with burning zeal by the next great king, Olav Tryggvason (the archetype of the Viking hero) with the help of English missionaries and a convincing supplement of strong-arm tactics. But in the year 1000, a Norwegian army of peasant-farmers, supported by the kings of Denmark and Sweden, attacked his realm. The crucial sea-battle that followed cost the king his life and Norway its unity. Although a large part of the land remained under the control of a Norwegian earl, the rest was divided up between Denmark and Sweden.

Thirty years later Norway's history took a decisive turn when Olav Haraldsson (another descendent of Harald Fairhair) died losing another battle. But now the country was ready for independence and despite the king's crude methods in rooting out pagan strongholds, his rule of law and Christian ideas were cherished. Attendant miracles at his grave were sufficient to confirm him in the hearts and minds of the Norwegian people as their saint. Thus the Norwegians were united and the Christian Church institutionalized throughout the land.

St. Olav's young son won the name Magnus the Good. He consolidated power and made peace with the Danes—in fact he ruled Denmark as well as Norway for a time. His successor, the dashing Harald Hardråde (meaning "hard ruler"), distinguished himself as a fearless warrior. He also takes credit for the founding of the city of Oslo. His long reign ended far away in Yorkshire, where the ambitious Norwegian king died contesting the crown of England on the battlefield at Stamford Bridge. The year was 1066.

During the 12th and 13th centuries, most of the news in Norway concerned church–state conflicts and struggles between rival claimants to the throne. At one time, two kings ruled simultaneously— Harald IV and Magnus IV; the latter went down in history as Magnus the Blind after Harald had him disposed of by, among other mutilations, blinding.

An example of a typical tussle of the time was the conflict between King Sverre and Archbishop Eric Ivarsson at the end of the 12th century. The king cut off the appropriation for the archbishop's bodyguard when the archbishop refused to crown him due to his illegitimacy. In return, the king was excommunicated by the Pope. For a while, the two sides (church vs. state) waged what amounted to a civil war.

The peacemaker, Håkon IV, was acclaimed king in 1217 and belatedly crowned by a papal representative 30 years later. It took the Vatican that long to decide on the legitimacy of his reign in view of his illegitimate birth.

During Håkon's long reign, Norway enjoyed enough prosperity to begin sharing in Europe's interests: friendship treaties were signed with other states; churches and cathedrals were built; European fashions were copied; the ideals of chivalry came into vogue. Norway's territorial ambitions reached their greatest fulfilment under Håkon IV. Then his son, Magnus VI, handed over the Hebrides and the Isle of Man to the King of Scotland, beginning the empire's decline. But Magnus, known as the Lawmender, bequeathed his country a constitution which included a sort of parliament, and he drew up a unified code of common law.

The 13th century kings gave special privileges to merchants from Germany's Baltic coast, who were the only reliable source of grain. But as Norway became increasingly dependent on the Hanseatic League, the traders came to enjoy disproportionate influence. By the 15th century, they controlled all Norway's foreign commerce and operated as a state within a state.

Norway in Eclipse

Bubonic plague ravaged Norway in the middle of the 14th century. Two-thirds of the population was estimated to have perished. With the farms unmanned and unproductive, survivors were also afflicted with hunger.

Combined with the natural calamity of the Black Death, political and economic setbacks undermined what remained of Norway's resistance to outside forces. The long story of Norway's relegation to dependent status began in 1319 when the Swedes elected the Norwegian king, Magnus Eriksson, to serve as their ruler as well. No sooner did this arrangement end than Norway fell into union with Denmark. Over most of the period from 1397 to 1521, one king ruled all the Scandinavian countries.

But Sweden's independent spirit finally triumphed, leaving Norway and Denmark a tensely mismatched couple. Norway was such a weak partner that in 1536 it was simply swallowed up and became part of the Kingdom of Denmark.

An event of even more lasting significance occurred in the same year, 1536: the Protestant Reformation reached Denmark, and soon after spread to the Danish province of Norway. At first the Catholic archbishop of Nidaros (now the city of Trondheim) mobilized for an armed struggle against both Denmark and Lutheranism, but he went into exile instead. Among the peasants, resistance to the reforms continued into the next century. Norway's new Lutheran bishops came from Denmark; so did the Bibles and hymnals, which were printed in Danish—a weighty influence, as it turned out, on the evolution of the Norwegian language.

By the end of the 16th century, Norway was beginning to make economic progress. The Hanseatic monopoly on foreign trade had been broken. The shipbuilding industry revived. Fish, timber and minerals became important exports. The centre of the fish trade, Bergen, was booming. Oslo, destroyed by a fire in 1624, was rebuilt according to a grand plan by the dynamic Danish King Christian IV. He called the town Christiania after himself. The name was to last until 1925 when it was changed back to Oslo.

Renaissance fortress of Akershus *dominates Oslo's dynamic harbour.*

Detached from Denmark

During the Napoleonic wars, Denmark (hence Norway) became involved on the losing side. Norway suffered a British blockade which not only ruined foreign trade, but actually led to famine. After Napoleon's defeat, the 1814 Treaty of Kiel forced Denmark to give up Norway to the Swedish crown.

As usual, nobody had consulted the Norwegians. Prominent citizens decided the time was ripe for Norway to stand alone. At a mansion in Eidsvoll, north of Oslo, 112 delegates assembled to draft a new constitution for an independent nation. They signed it on May 17, 1814. But scarcely six months later, the Great Powers railroaded Norway into union with Sweden. It was a blow to those long-simmering hopes for independence, but at least the constitution promulgated at Eidsvoll remained in force. Thus May 17 came to be celebrated as the national holiday of Norway, even though almost a century was **21** to pass before nationhood was finally achieved.

Predictably, frictions developed in the union between Sweden and its involuntary junior partner. For several years Norway was deprived of its own flag. Sweden insisted on handling Norway's diplomatic relations, causing frustrations which were to become critical. Meanwhile, population growth outstripped the expansion of the Norwegian economy. In the decade after the American Civil War, more than 100,000 Norwegians emigrated, mostly to the U.S. They tended to seek out places where the terrain or climate reminded them of home—Minnesota, Wisconsin, Washington state. By the start of World War I, a total of three-quarters of a million had left Norway to seek a livelihood abroad.

Independence

Years of conflict between Norway and Sweden came to a head in 1905 when Stockholm vetoed Norwegian plans to set up a separate consular service. Prime Minister Christian Michelsen, a Bergen shipowner, decided this was the do-or-die issue. Norway's parliament, the Storting, agreed and voted to end the union with Sweden. Oscar II, King of Sweden and Norway, was pained by the act of rejection, which would cost him half his realm. A plebiscite was ordered. Norwegian voters left no room for doubt: they ratified independence by a margin of 2,000 to 1.

The Norwegian government chose a new king, the tall, young Prince Carl of Denmark; his wife, Princess Maud, was the daughter of Britain's King Edward VII. With heavy emphasis on continuity, the new monarch assumed the name of Haakon VII. His predecessor, Håkon VI, last king of an independent Norway had died in 1380.

Between independence and the outbreak of the First World War, abundant hydroelectric power fuelled Norway's big leap forward as an industrial nation. When war came to Europe, Scandinavia asserted its neutrality. Though some businessmen reaped quick profits from the war raging outside, the great majority of the citizens—like the national economy—entered the 1920s in worse shape than before the war. Hard times nudged the political balance to the left, and in the depression year of 1933, the

Natural riches: drying stockfish, converting water into electricity.

Labour Party won 40 per cent of the vote. Labour came to power in 1935, and the foundations of a planned economy were laid.

World War II

Norway's traditional neutrality failed to head off tragedy in World War II. Germany invaded on April 9, 1940. Less than two months later, with the German steamroller unstoppable, the king and the government fled from the Norwegian arctic to continue the fight from London.

Only hours after the invasion, the leader of Norway's pro-Nazi party, Vidkun Quisling, proclaimed himself prime minister, although the party had polled less than 2 per cent of the votes at the previous election. Under the Nazis, Quisling as *ministerpresident* of Norway tried to run a government of collaborators. Captured leaders of the underground were executed and about 35,000 Norwegians were sent to concentration camps before the fortunes of war turned.

Unprecedented jubilation overwhelmed Norway on May 7, 1945, when the Germans surrendered to the allied forces. King Haakon returned to Oslo on June 7, five years to the day after sailing into exile. The courts decreed the execution of 25 Nazi collaborators, headed by Vidkun Quisling, the jowly Norwegian whose name had become a common noun meaning 'traitor'.

When Foreign Minister Trygve Lie became the first secretary-general of the United Nations, Norway took an active role in peace-keeping efforts. The nation's foreign relations reached historic turning points, when the country joined the North Atlantic Treaty Organization in 1949; and, in 1972, after a closely decided referendum, decided *not* to join the European Economic Community.

In 1957, after a reign of more than half a century, King Haakon VII died. His son, Olav V—namesake of Norway's national saint—assumed the throne of a country well on its way to recovery from the war's deep wounds. Since then, industrial expansion has been notable. But the most sensational development came in the 70s, when immense offshore oil and gas deposits were discovered and exploited. They posed a novel challenge: how to keep a gusher of prosperity under control. It's the sort of problem many a less fortunate nation would be happy to have to solve.

Where to Go

Getting to know a country the size of Norway takes a lot more than one holiday. After a first superficial look, many tourists return another year to dig deeper within the zones they liked best, or spread out in search of new discoveries.

This book concentrates on the most-visited areas—Oslo and Bergen and the Western Fjords. Almost every place mentioned can be reached by public transport, which encompasses trams, buses, trains, and boats of many sizes. You can drive most of it yourself. Or you can sign on for various tours by coach or combinations of bus, train and boat.

Depending on your interests and how much time you have, how you want to travel and where to start and finish, the permutations are almost limitless. So we try to avoid hard-and-fast itineraries. But for convenience of organization we start in Oslo, then cross to Norway's second city, Bergen, before striking out for the best-known fjords. Along the way we offer diversions for those with time to spare, ending with some notes about the unforgettable Coastal Express cruise which only a few voyagers are lucky enough to experience.

Oslo

Geologists come to admire Oslo's foundations. These ancient rocks are some of the oldest on the face of the earth, dating back hundreds of millions of years. But as European capitals go, it's quite a late-bloomer. Though it was founded more than 900 years ago, Oslo had a population of fewer than 10,000 at the turn of the 19th century, smaller than Bergen. Today slightly less than half a million people live here. Ironically, it's still one of the world's largest cities with an area of 175 square miles, consisting mainly of forests and farmland. Skiers and hikers don't have to leave town, and botanists can enjoy more than a thousand species of wild plants within the city limits.

The first king to be crowned in Oslo, Håkon V (who ruled from 1299 to 1319), built Akershus Castle overlooking the harbour. For a perspective of the town and a taste of its history, there's no better place to start a tour of Oslo than at the castle. And from here all the centre of the city can be explored on foot.

Even the names of some parts of **Akershus Slott og Festning** conjure up images of derring-do, chivalry and strife: The Daredevil's Tower, the Dark Passage, and Knut's Tower (named after the leader of an unsuccessful revolt, whose body was displayed there as a warning to others). The medieval castle was expanded, renovated and further fortified by Christian IV, who exerted paramount influence over 17th century Oslo.

Sculpture softens severity of Rådhuset, *controversial red-brick town hall inaugurated in 1950, the 900th anniversary of the foundation of Oslo.*

When fire almost totally destroyed the old wooden town in 1624, the king came up with a crash programme to rebuild it in brick and stone on a new site, much better protected from potential invaders because of its proximity to the fortress. Oslo's name was changed to Christiania. The original name probably derived from the Old Norse words for "the Gods' Glade". Few of Christiania's original buildings remain, but the street plan is a relic of that 17th century blueprint.

The complexities of Akershus Castle are best understood by taking one of the several daily guided tours to see the historical and architectural details—secret passages, dungeons, royal halls and the modern royal crypt. The castle is still used for state occasions; the recently restored Olav Hall comfortably seats more than 100 guests at banquets.

Though often besieged Akershus actually fell only once—to the Germans in World War II. It became headquarters of the occupation troops. In the grounds a simple monument honours 37 resistance fighters executed on the spot: "They fought, they fell, they gave us their all."

Alongside this poignant stone, **Norges Hjemmefrontmuseum** (the Norwegian Resistance Movement Museum) is filled with heartbreaking evidence of wartime suffering. You can read life-and-death documents and hear the recorded voices of King Haakon, Winston Churchill and the sinister Quisling.

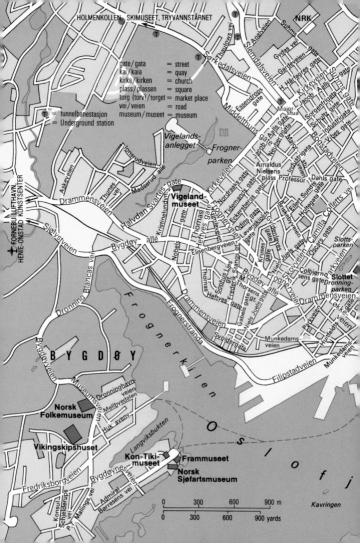

HOLMENKOLLEN, SKIMUSEET, TRYVANNSTÅRNET

NRK

gate/gata = street
kai/kaia = quay
kirke/kirken = church
plass/plassen = square
torg (torv)/torget = market place
vei/veien = road
museum/museet = museum

T = tunnelbanestasjon
= Underground station

Sørkedalsveien

Vigelands-
anlegget
Frogner-
parken

Amaldus
Nielsens
plass Professor Dahls gate

Vigeland-
museet

FORNEBU LUFTHAVN
HENIE-ONSTAD KUNSTSENTER

Drammensveien

Bygdøy allé

Slottet

Dronning-
parken

Slotts-
parken

B Y G D Ø Y

Frognerkilen

Frognerstranda

Munkedams-
veien

Filipstadveien

Munkedams-
veien

Norsk
Folkemuseum

Vikingskipshuset

Kon-Tiki-
museet

Frammuseet

Norsk
Sjøfartsmuseum

O s l o f j

Kavringen

Fredriksborgveien

0   300   600   900 m

0   300   600   900 yards

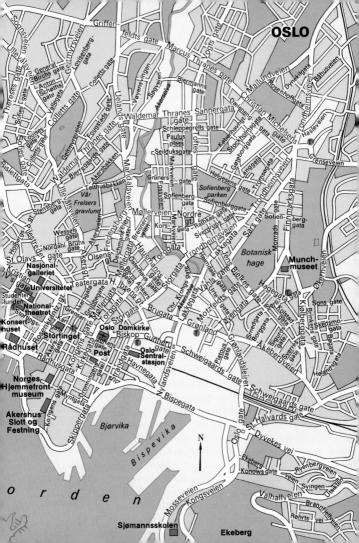

A newer museum at Akershus, **Forsvarsmuseet** (Armed Forces Museum) traces the history of Norway's military from the days of swords to the jet age.

From the battlements of Akershus the **view** over the harbour and the centre of Oslo takes in a lively scene of ships' cranes, ferryboats, islands and the unmistakable form of the 20th-century **Rådhuset** (the Town Hall). Critics of this controversial building say its twin towers have the shape and colour of those square goat-cheeses found on Norwegian breakfast tables. For better or worse, the heavy structure is covered with 1½-million hand-made bricks. All manner of decoration—sculpture, frieze and abstract embellishment—is mobilized to relieve the ponderous effect. Inside,

Karl Johans gate, capital's main street, leads from parliament to palace; opposite: bronze reliefs on door of 17th-century cathedral, Oslo Domkirke.

many of the walls are covered with modern narrative murals. There is so much to see in all the gala public rooms that it's worthwhile joining one of the free guided tours. Even if you arrive out of hours, be sure to inspect the courtyard surrounding the main entrance. Notice the fountain of swans, the puzzling astronomical clock and the polychrome wood reliefs of themes from Norse mythology. Sightseeing bus tours and cruises start from the harbour side of the town hall.

West of the town hall, the quayside **Aker Brygge** complex incorporates offices, flats, restaurants and shops. A spectacular waterfront setting and some lively special events make this a focus for urban living.

Inland, a few streets behind the town hall, the urban scene opens out to reveal public gardens, a spacious strolling zone in the very heart of Oslo. At the western extreme, along with a bandstand and an outdoor café, stands the National Theatre. The statues outside depict two of the country's literary luminaries—Henrik Ibsen and his contemporary, Nobel prizewinner Bjørnstjerne Bjørnson. This area is called **Studenterlunden** (the Students' Grove) because the 19th century buildings of Oslo

University are just across the street, **Karl Johans gate***.

This is the main street of the capital. The eastern end of it

---

* *Gate*, often abbreviated *gt.*, is Norwegian for "street", not "gate". **31**

Smartly uniformed sentry struts across Royal Palace grounds as three more guards wait their turn.

becomes a pedestrian precinct. Strollers here stop to watch an unpredictable cast of impromptu entertainers—folksingers, mimes and fire-eaters.

The parliament building, Stortinget, is an exceedingly sober brick structure facing Karl Johan's Street. Though parliament was established in 1814, the legislators didn't have a proper meeting place to call their own until this palace was opened in the 1860s.

Several blocks east of Stortinget, **Oslo Domkirke** (Oslo Cathedral) was consecrated in 1697, replacing a church destroyed by a fire blamed on a lightning bolt. The lofty turreted tower which glints over central Oslo was designed by a German architect, inspired by a Danish castle. It was added to the skyline in 1850, one of the key years in the history of the Church of Our Saviour (as it was called until 1950). To the right of the main entrance, notice the startling stone sculpture built into the brick wall. Showing a man under attack by monsters, the relief is thought to have been salvaged from the ruins of the medieval St. Hallvard's Cathedral. It was probably carved about the year 1100.

The interior of the present cathedral successfully combines Baroque and 20th century elements. An unidentified Dutch master of the late 17th century was responsible for the majestic circular pulpit and the intricately carved altarpiece. The royal pew has perched diagonally opposite from the pulpit since the earliest days of the church, though it has been remodelled several times. The ceiling was painted in tempera by Hugo Louis Mohr between 1936 and 1950; biblical stories are pictured in straightforward modern style.

Walk back west on Karl Johan's Street to get to **Slottet**, the Royal Palace on the hill. Without an invitation you can't tour Slottet, but the fine park surrounding the palace is always open to the pub-lic. The sentries, royal guardsmen with black horsetail plumes on their hats, are always a good subject for a photograph. The most exciting time to be here is on May 17, Constitution Day. The royal family stands on the classical balcony reviewing an endless and enthusiastic parade of school children. For a good view of the royalty—and the kids—be sure to arrive before 10 a.m. This is no place to find yourself at the back of a crowd; the Norwegians are too tall to overlook.

Museums

Most of Oslo's museums (over 30 of them) deal with Norwegian themes—historical, artistic and maritime. Five of the best are grouped within walking distance of one another on the Bygdøy peninsula south-west of central Oslo, easily reached by bus or ferryboat. Going to Bygdøy by car is easy enough but finding a parking space is not. It would take prodigious determination as well as energy to do justice to all five museums in a single day; don't even try it.

Vikingskipshuset (the Viking Ship Museum). Built like a very severe-looking modern church, this museum enshrines three authentic **33**

Viking ships. Bigger and more beautiful than any other relics of the Norsemen, these wooden vessels survived about 1,000 years because they had been forgotten for centuries under airtight layers of stone, clay and dirt. The ships had served as tombs for royal or aristocratic personages. Even though grave robbers stripped the burial chambers of almost everything that glittered, enough artefacts were left to prove how artistic the Vikings could be. Some of the richest finds are on view in the fourth wing of the museum—haunting sculptures, a wonderfully embellished cart and sleighs.

The low-lying **Oseberg Ship**, built in the early 9th century, was unearthed at Oseberg, in the Oslo Fjord district, in 1904. With a length of 70 feet, it was designed to be a ceremonial barge or pleasure boat rather than a flagship for expeditions on the high seas. The precision of the shipbuilders, who had to work with iron-age tools, and the artistry of the wood-carvers are most remarkable. In the burial chamber were found the remains of two women, one thought to be Queen Asa, the other her servant—presumably honoured to be slain for the occasion.

An even bigger ship, the *Gokstad* discovered down the fjord at Sandar, looks less decorative and more seaworthy. And indeed a careful replica was built and sailed across the North Atlantic in 1893 to attend the Chicago World's Fair.

The third ship was excavated in 1867 at Tune, on the east side of the Oslo Fjord. It was badly damaged by decay. In this case, instead of trying to restore the ship, experts decided to put it on display in its incomplete state to reveal inner details of the construction. The final mission of the Tune Ship was as the tomb of an unidentified Viking, presumably an important chieftain; he was buried with his horse.

Norsk Folkemuseum (Norwegian Folk Museum), neighbouring the Viking Ship Museum, is a vast permanent exhibition showing the way town and country people lived over recent centuries. More than 150 old buildings have been removed from various parts of the country and reassembled in this attractive park. They cover all aspects of rural architecture from farmhouses and barns to lofts and even outdoor toilets. Here you can see one of the oldest surviving wooden

Oslo museums chronicle centuries of seafaring, Vikings to Ra II.

Close-up view: haunting themes of Edvard Munch fill Oslo museum.

houses in Norway, from the 13th-century, with a runic inscription above the door. And here a **stave church** from the same era was restored. Only a couple of dozen of these tall wooden churches still stand in Norway, the survivors of fire, decay or sheer indifference. The dragon-shaped projections on the roofs (to ward off evil spirits)

urban life, peasant and religious art. One unusual display is a re-creation of the spacious study of the Oslo home of Henrik Ibsen. After working as artistic director of the former Christiania Norwegian Theatre in Oslo, the playwright went abroad. He spent his most productive years in Italy and Germany, stirring up scandals and sensations with immortal dramas like *A Doll's House, An Enemy of the People* and *Hedda Gabler*. He returned to Oslo for the last 17 years of his life, dying in 1906 at the ripe old age of 78.

The three remaining museums of Bygdøy, all on nautical themes, are clustered on the waterfront, perhaps a 15-minute walk from the Folk Museum.

Kon-Tiki-museet commemorates the voyages of the daring Norwegian ethnologist Thor Heyerdahl. In 1947 he built the primitive balsa raft *Kon-Tiki* in Peru and sailed it to Polynesia, to show that the ancient South Americans could have contributed to the culture of Pacific peoples. *Kon-Tiki* is on display, along with the reed ship *Ra II*, used for Heyerdahl's 1970 expedition across the Atlantic. The giant Easter Island statue peering down onto *Kon-Tiki* is only a copy.

Fram-museet. In 1935 the veteran polar exploration ship *Fram*

are typical of stave churches; they may indicate that the early Christians, still so close to pagan times, were hedging their bets.

Several large buildings complement the outdoor exhibit, housing collections on such themes as was hauled ashore at Bygdøy and a museum was built around it. In the Fram Museum you can walk around, over and all through this historic 800-tonner, the flagship of two great Norwegian explorers, Fridtjof Nansen and Roald Amundsen. Specially built to resist the strain of the ice pack, in fact to be lifted up onto the ice by its force, *Fram* is the only ship to have come so close to both the north and south poles. Notice the human touches from the years the crew spent cloistered aboard—Nansen's cabin with its memorabilia, the polar fur costumes, the piano in the officers' mess.

Norsk Sjøfartsmuseum (Norwegian Maritime Museum), next to the Fram Museum, concentrates on the less glamorous side of the sea—the workaday vessels which have made Norway one of the world's most important fishing and shipping powers. There are ship models galore, graphic details of whaling expeditions, and a working radar's view of Oslo's harbour traffic.

Back in the centre of town, **Nasjonalgalleriet** (the National Gallery), founded in 1836, contains a cross-section of European art. Predictably the greatest emphasis falls on Norwegian artists, including contemporary painters and sculptors. Among the great Norwegian artists, look for the landscapes of Johan Christian Dahl, the rural landscapes of Erik Werenskiold, the social comment of Harriet Backer and Christian Krohg. Norway's greatest painter, Edvard Munch, is well represented, even though a separate Oslo museum is devoted to him (see below). The National Gallery also has a creditable collection of French Impressionists as well as an El Greco, a David and a couple of Rembrandts.

Munch-museet (the Munch Museum), in an area of parks in eastern Oslo, is a high-spot for art-lovers. This engaging modern institution contains the life work which Edvard Munch bequeathed to the city. It was opened in 1963 on the centenary of his birth. The reserve of paintings, etchings and lithographs is many times larger than the walls can hold, so exhibitions are periodically changed. But you'll always be able to see a cross-section of the work of this powerful artist on display. He's best known for his haunted, tragic figures and original colours. Many of Munch's themes reflect the strains of his own unhappy life: his mother died of tuberculosis when he was five, then a sister died, and another sister went mad. His self-portraits, from youth to old age, many painted when he was anguished, provide additional insight into this pacesetter of 20th-century expressionism. Acclaimed but still controversial, he died in 1944, in his 81st year.

Vigelandsanlegget (the Vigeland Sculpture Park), in Frogner Park in west Oslo, is the biggest one-man show you've ever seen—almost all the works ever produced by Gustav Vigeland (1869–1943), a compulsively busy sculptor. In 1921, he gave all his statues to the city in exchange for a studio in which to produce them, some assistants, living quarters and a small stipend.

The studio, outside the park, to the south is now **Vigelandmuseet**, a museum crammed with thou-

Sculpture park displays prodigious life's work of Gustav Vigeland.

sands of his sculptures, drawings and plans. It all contributes greatly to an understanding of this artist and the problems of a sculptor's work.

In the park, Vigeland tries to cover all aspects of human life from childhood to extreme old age. There are some 200 statues of children and men and women doing all, or almost all, the things they do in real life, alone or together. Vigeland's last work, towering over this vast outdoor exhibit, is a monolith composed, like some oriental puzzle, of 121 intertwined human figures.

Another imaginative statue by Vigeland stands in Slottsparken, near the Royal Palace. The title, Abel, refers not to Cain's brother but to Niels Henrik Abel (1802–1829), Norway's boy genius of mathematics.

Located at Høvikodden, some 6 miles south-west of Oslo, is the **Henie-Onstad Kunstsenter** (Art Centre). Set up by the world-famous skating champion Sonja Henie and her shipbuilder husband, the collection includes paintings by Munch, Bonnard, Picasso, Miró and post-war pictures of the French abstract school. A special room contains the countless trophies and medals won by Sonja Henie during her years as reigning ice queen. The centre arranges film showings, concerts, ballet and theatre performances.

Norway Travel Association

Daredevil skiers fly through the air at 50 miles per hour from famous Holmenkollen Ski-Jump,
40 *scene of popular annual festival.*

Noteworthy too, is the modern building housing the centre, aluminium and glass spread like a hand over a lovely promontory by the Oslo Fjord.

Perspectives

Nowadays every town, even the ones without much to look at, seems to have a TV tower with a viewing platform. Oslo is no exception to this municipal conceit, but at least the panorama is noteworthy.

Tryvannstårnet (the Tryvann Tower) has an observation platform, reached by express lift, which boosts your point of view to

an altitude of more than 1,700 feet above sea level. The view extends over an area estimated at about 11,500 square miles—as far as the Swedish border. The tower stands within walking distance of the Voksenkollen station on Holmenkolbanen, the suburban railway which starts at the underground station just behind the National Theatre.

Holmenkollen Ski-Jump. This frighteningly high ski-jump in west Oslo has a view and a history of its own, plus a museum on the premises. For a century Norwegian daredevils have been flying through the air at Holmenkollen, last rebuilt and improved in 1980. The Olympics of 1952 brought out a crowd of 130,000 fans. For a few kroner you can use the self-service lift to the top of the ski-jump. If you're queasy about heights this may not be for you. The skier's-eye view down the runway into the great beyond might make a competitor prefer to walk back down. Mere sightseers, who can look forward to a safe ride back to earth without shame, will consider the panorama of Oslo and its fjord a good investment of time and money.

Skimuseet, snuggling beneath the jump, displays some unusual evidence to prove that skiing was invented in Norway: a 2,000-year-old ski found at Alvdal, north of Oslo. Other historical exhibits show the rather hit-or-miss evolution of skis, boots, bindings and poles over the years. You can see a 19th-century Sámi sleigh (it was reindeer-propelled), a sled from the Amundsen South Pole expedition and skis used by the Norwegian royal family, who are still avid skiers.

Another vantage point over Oslo, **Ekeberg**, is a few minutes' tram ride east of the centre of town. The park here, Oslo's biggest, includes sports facilities and hundreds of acres of forest.

From the **Merchant Marine Academy** (*Sjømannsskolen*) below the park, you get a mapmaker's prospect of the island-speckled inner fjord and an idea of the extent of maritime activity here—for business as well as pleasure. Inside the building is an important fresco painting by Per Krohg, and in the grounds a striking sculpture, the *Hell Horse*, by Gunnar Utsond. Behind the academy, beyond a low fence, see the designs described as 5,000-year-old carvings in the sloping rock. Most of them depict four-footed animals.

Another perspective of Oslo is the view from the sea. The **Oslo Fjord**, Norway's third largest fjord in area, stretches for about 60 miles from the Skagerrak to the harbour of Oslo. Cruise-ship passengers and car-ferry trippers from Copenhagen or Kiel can see it all. For a condensed version, take one of the two-hour harbour tours which leave the quay at city hall several times a day.

The red brick Town Hall is one of the landmarks which lingers in view. So does Akershus Castle and most of all the ski-jump at Holmenkollen (standing out like a stiletto-heeled white shoe).

If the word *fjord* suggests cliffs containing a narrow waterway, the Oslo Fjord fails to match the stereotype. The shore is mostly flat, though appealing green islands and rocky outcrops thronged with argumentative gulls enliven the scenery. Some of the islands are bases for professional fishing fleets but most host weekend anglers and sailors. Parked just off Bygdøy, white and scrubbed, you'll usually find the eminently sea-worthy royal yacht *Norge*. The profusion of pleasure boats in this area shows how easy it is for Oslo residents to escape the pressures of city life.

The Bergen Railway

When it first opened for traffic in 1909, the *Bergensbanen* was considered an amazing engineering achievement. A journey on the line, from Oslo to the west coast, still feels that way, particularly for the type of passenger who strains to "help" the train up steep inclines and round tight bend. The high-spot of the trip—quite awesome in any season—is the hour rolling above the timberline in a terrain so hostile that you can sense the struggle it must have been to build and maintain this single iron link.

In all, *Bergensbanen* is 292 miles long. The highest point is 4,268 feet above sea level—scarcely worth mentioning in many countries, but an appalling altitude to be at here in the north, where waist-high snow-drifts linger into June. About 200 tunnels had to be blasted through the mountains to build the railway. Seventeen miles of snow-sheds make the trip possible year-round.

The first half of the journey from Oslo covers relatively easy ground from the engineering standpoint, and it's easy on the eyes. But soon the scene changes to wild forests and primitive lakes. On a warm **43**

summer day those lakes can look diabolically inviting.

On the way to the tersely named small town of FLÅ, the railway twists and turns high above the banks of the long, sinuous Lake Krøderen. White and black sheep graze on the steep hillsides. Though the altitude is still low, the hills are rocky and rugged: trees bravely sprout from the thinnest patches of earth. For mile after mile, the only sign that the country is inhabited may be the pylons carrying high-tension wires to far-off customers of Norway's hydroelectric industry.

At the village of TORPO across the river from the right-of-way, the passengers get a glimpse of a 12th-century stave church, dedicated to St. Margaret. The next station bears the most economical name of all for the railway's sign-painters: ÅL, which means "nar-

Along the Bergen Railway: in summer, grass is hung on wires to dry; winter is long and harsh in the mountains near snow capital of Finse.

row river valley". Soon the train is climbing steadily, with snow clad mountains in the distance, until **Geilo**, a leading ski centre. Most of Geilo's hotels are open year-round. The skiing season lasts from Christmas until at least April.

For the next 45 minutes, the train strains uphill past the last stunted birch trees into a land of utter desolation. The profusion of tunnels, snow-sheds, snow fences and makeshift barricades gives even the midsummer traveller an indication of the yearly battle to keep the line open. It was far worse for the men who built the railway, who had to import even the firewood to keep them from freezing. On the really bad days they worked inside the tunnels.

Norway's highest railway station, FINSE, claims an altitude of nearly 4,010 feet. The hamlet's principal industry is snow removal. This may appear to be a seasonal occupation, but in the few months between crises the ploughs must be maintained and the snow fences reinforced.

Beyond Finse, Hardangerjøkulen glacier stretches alongside the railway; this is where the English explorer Robert Falcon Scott trained for his 1912 expedition to the South Pole.

Approaching the town of MYRDAL, on the beginning of the downhill stretch, openings in the tunnel wall give brief views onto an enchanting valley. Some passengers disembark at Myrdal to take the side-trip down to sealevel at Flåm on one of the world's most sensational branch railway lines (see pp. 61–62).

Beyond Myrdal on the main line is the longest tunnel of all—nearly 3½ miles burrowed beneath rock, snow and ice. If you don't like confined spaces, this will be the place to take a nap.

The next stop, MJØLFJELL, is a winter sports resort. Inspiring scenery—forests of birch, spruce and fir, waterfalls and rushing rivers—continues until **Voss**, a major tourist resort and educational centre. In addition to its splendid lake and mountain setting, Voss takes pride in its historic monuments. Finneloftet, the oldest secular structure of wood still standing in Norway, was a banquet hall in the Middle Ages; Voss Church, of stone, was built in the 13th century; nearby, a stone cross commemorates the conversion of the town to Christianity in 1023.

Heading west from Voss, the spectacular scenery continues. The track follows a river course through narrow valleys bracketed by steep green hills. Sometimes the valley is wide enough for a few houses and a road as well as the railway track, but the route is often as narrow as a trench. It all climaxes in a classic fjord scene, with cliffs plunging to the waterline and one bend of the fjord revealing the next.

One last, very long tunnel, and the knowledgeable travellers begin putting on coats and collecting baggage. It's only a matter of a minute or two to the terminal at Bergen, a delightful seafaring town with its own unmistakable atmosphere.

Bergen

Until the railway opened in 1909, Bergen's citizens could get to London more quickly than to Oslo. This is one of the reasons why Bergen is so different. As an ancient trading town facing west, it had contacts abroad that Oslo never had. Today, Bergen is an up-to-date, prosperous town of over 200,000 inhabitants with a passionate interest in its past. Its prized medieval wooden buildings bristle with fire-extinguishers and automatic sprinkler systems to ensure their permanent survival. Great fires have plagued Bergen over the centuries despite the town's frequent rains.

Bergen was founded in 1070 and quickly became a centre of trade with Iceland, the Shetlands, Orkneys and the north of Norway. During the 13th century, five kings were crowned in Bergen's old cathedral. But when Oslo began to take precedence, Bergen drifted into the sphere of influence of the Hanseatic League. Business boomed and culture took a distant second place to commerce. Still, Bergen was dynamic and cosmopolitan and always a favourite with fishermen, seamen and travellers from far away.

If you arrive today on a cruise liner, you'll disembark at the seaward end of the narrow, crowded inner harbour. Freighters, ferries and visiting yachts share this sanctuary right in the heart of town. In many ways it still looks like 17th-century prints of Bergen. For instance, **Bergenhus**, the fortress guarding the north-east side of the port, has been restored to its medieval look.

The gem of Bergenhus, the step-gabled **Håkonshallen** (Håkon's Hall), is a 700-year-old monument any town would be proud of. It served as the ceremonial hall of a burgeoning Norwegian empire. The first great occasion celebrated in Håkonshallen was the marriage in 1261 of King Magnus Håkonsson (the Lawmender) and Princess Ingeborg of Denmark. We are told that the invitation list contained more than a thousand names—royalty, ecclesiastics and townsfolk. The party went on for three days and nights.

In 1944, along with virtually all harbourside buildings, Håkonshallen was ravaged by an explosion and fire. A German ammunition ship, moored alongside the fortress in defiance of safety regulations, blew up with the loss of more than 100 lives. The cause

BERGEN

of the disaster was neither Nazi skulduggery nor Resistance sabotage. The big blow-up was an accident—spontaneous combustion in the fuel bunkers. After the war, during the reconstruction of Håkonshallen, tasteful modern interior decoration and conveniences were added to make the hall a comfortable year-round venue for concerts or banquets.

Rosenkrantztårnet (Rosenkrantz Tower) is named after a powerful 16th century governor of Bergen, Erik Rosenkrantz. He recruited a Scottish architect, stonecutters and masons to create an impressive Renaissance castle around a nucleus of 13th-century fortifications. Through a maze of grand halls, narrow passageways and spiral staircases, you finally reach the battlements around the roof, covered with immense slate slabs. From here you survey the seaport from the same vantage point the 16th-century artillerymen enjoyed. The onion dome, topped with a weathervane, is a reconstruction based on drawings and descriptions from 400 years ago.

East of Bergenhus, **Mariakirken** (St. Mary's Church), is a treasure built in the 12th century and stocked with glorious medieval works of art. Like most buildings of such great age, St. Mary's suffered some accidents over the years, including a couple of ruinous fires in the Middle Ages. But it's almost unchanged since the great fire of 1248; even the Protestant Reformation had little effect, although most other Bergen churches, including the old cathedral, were either destroyed or abandoned. Mariakirken was the parish church of the Hansa merchants and thus protected. To this day it's also known as Tyskekirken (the German church). St. Mary's is one of the few triple-naved stone churches in Norway, and the only one with twin square towers on the west front. The triptych, a North German work from the end of the 15th century, has been restored to its original brilliance; other fine paintings line the walls. The pulpit, imported from an untraceable source in the 17th century, is a Baroque masterpiece.

Across the street from the church, **Schøtstuene** (the Assembly Rooms), offer a revealing glimpse of life inside the Hanseatic League. The big "club room" with grand fireplaces was the only room heated even on the coldest days, for fires were prohibited elsewhere on safety grounds. The merchants and apprentices, who **49**

what was the heart of medieval Bergen. This whole district is Bergen's most distinctive architectural asset. Many of the typical steeply gabled wooden buildings were burned down over the centuries. After a fire in 1955 levelled five of the remaining structures, researchers followed firemen into the rubble. The archaeologists left no stone unturned in the search for understanding how people lived in medieval Bergen. Some of the results, often with an unconventional human angle, are displayed in the museum.

The surviving buildings line the inner end of the port. *Bryggen*, sometimes called Tyskebryggen (the German Wharf), was the domain of the Hansa merchants from the middle of the 14th century till the Reformation's early years. The houses are still in use, for a variety of purposes: offices, restaurants and artisans' workshops.

The **Hanseatic Museum** on the quay has the last word on that epoch. In one of the original houses, you can wander at will amidst a jumble of relics. You can see the apprentices' sleeping quarters, spartan even by the standards of a respectable dog kennel. And look through the wavy old glass of the windows onto the port and fish market.

had to abide by the most rigid rules, lived and worked in extremely close quarters. Even skylights and chandeliers barely ease the gloom in these buildings.

Bryggens Museum, a new museum of archaeology, was cleverly **50** built right on top of the "digs" in

Bergen's harbourside **market**, surrounded by history, may lack some of the noise and animation of outdoor bazaars in warmer climates, but the goods on sale couldn't be better presented. The fish are laid out as scrubbed and straight as cadets on parade—fresh whole mackerel, meaty fillets of salmon, dried cod, prawns galore. Nearby, big tanks keep fish alive for the buyers who like them extra fresh. They're flapping about in cold brine, crammed together like bathers in a nightmare swimming-pool, waiting to be chosen for the chop.

Elsewhere in the cheerful, roomy market-place are fruit and vegetable stands with delicacies year round, and a big section of prettily arranged flowers and plants.

In historic Bergen: a 17th-century pulpit in Mariakirken; *a street of carefully preserved Hansa houses.*

The local tourist information office, in the middle of the extra-wide shopping precinct called **Torgalmenning**, distributes maps and brochures and sells sightseeing-tour tickets. Keeping time with the midnight sun, it stays open until 11 p.m. all summer. The monument at the fish-market end of Torgalmenning honours the memory of Norwegian sailors who perished at sea. In addition to all the ordinary benches set out for weary shoppers and travellers, notice the special first-class bench with its own mosaic pavement. This is where the mayor of Bergen meets his constituents at regular intervals—an intimate, outdoor version of a town meeting.

The boulevard called Ole Bulls Plass leads uphill to **Den Nationale Scene** (the National Stage), a century-old theatre. Bergen is the birthplace of Norwegian drama. Until the first Norwegian-language theatre opened here in 1850, dramas were customarily performed in Danish. In 1852, an aspiring playwright named Henrik Ibsen, aged 23, was hired as an author-producer at Bergen's new theatre. The local man for whom this boulevard is named, Ole Bull, is commemorated in a fanciful monument in the tiny park facing

the Hotel Norge. One of the founders of the National Theatre, Bull was an internationally known virtuoso violinist.

Appropriately, the municipal bandstand is near at hand. Outdoor concerts are often presented here, even in the rain (an even more

Reminders of Bergen's medieval greatness: warehouses unchanged since German traders held sway.

frequent feature of Bergen than concerts). Also appropriately facing the bandstand is a statue of Bergen's most famous son, Edvard Grieg. His music is inescapable in his hometown; there is even a daily recital (in summer) of his piano pieces. For information and tickets ask at the tourist office.

More Museums and Sights

Northern Europe's biggest **aquarium**, in a park overlooking the harbour, merits a visit any time, but try to be there at 11 a.m. or 2 p.m. or 6 p.m. That's when the penguins and seals are fed in their pool at the entrance to the institution. The feeding schedule is well known; even the local seagulls know when to swoop in and try to intercept some of the small

Bergeners, past and present: statues symbolic of local history stand above townsfolk taking the mild northern sun in Torgalmenning precinct.

fish being tossed to the amiable animals. Inside, there are remarkable displays of living coral and a big tank full of deadly piranha, all looking as harmless as felons asking time off for good behaviour. The aquarium sells a booklet explaining the establishment's layout and featuring colour pictures of the most prominent members of the underwater cast, including a handy glossary of marine fish in five languages.

For another angle on fish, visit **Fiskerimuseet** (the Fishery Museum), reflecting Bergen's age-old tradition as a centre of the fishing industry: see models of old sailing boats, along with antique hooks, knives and nets and 20th-century harpoon-guns the size of howitzers. The Fishery Museum shares a building (at Nordahl Brunsgate 9) with **Vestlandske Kunstindustrimuseum** (the Museum of Arts and Crafts), devoted to furniture, silver, ceramics, fabrics, costumes, toys and antique household gadgets. On the ground floor is a surprise hoard of hundreds of valuable items of Chinese art, some dating back more than a thousand years—statues, ceramics, scrolls and paintings.

Not far away, in the direction of the University uphill is **Sjøfartsmuseet** (Bergen Maritime Museum), an informative, pleasant place stocked with ship models from Viking times to the supertanker era ... and ships in bottles, too. Among life-sized, authentic souvenirs of the sea are real hawsers and prow ornaments, and ships' wheels and furnishings from the days of luxury liners. From the "Promenade Deck", floored with deck planks, there's a view out over the Dokkeskjær quay, part of Bergen's port.

Historisk Museum (Historical Museum), next door to the Maritime Museum, occupies a building described as a fine example of 20th century Neo-Romanticism. So abundant is the collection that the ground floor is devoted exclusively to exhibits from prehistoric Norway. The late Iron Age includes the Vikings, represented here by items of everyday life as well as opulent jewellery. Above-stairs, be sure to see the excellent collection of medieval religious art, including most of the medieval church altars still preserved in Norway. The institution's top two floors are devoted to Norwegian folk art and exotic ethnographical displays from faraway cultures.

Art lovers will want to spare some time for the museums along the south side of the octagonal seawater lake called Lille Lungegårdsvann. A discreet new building mobilizes every bit of natural light to enhance the works on show in Bergen Billedgalleri (the municipal art museum) and Stenersens Samling (Stenersen's Collection). All the Norwegian masters and modern artists are represented; and from abroad Klee, Miró and a wall full of Picassos.

A few steps away, **Rasmus Meyers Samlinger** (Rasmus Meyer's Collection) is devoted to Norwegian painters. Enthusiasts of Edvard Munch will find paintings, etchings, lithographs and drawings galore here. And look for the revealing portraits of Hans Heyerdahl and Per Krohg, Harriet Backer's scenes of church and home life, Henrik Sørensen's country folk and inscrutable nudes, and the romantic landscapes of Johan Christian Dahl.

Across the street behind this museum stands **Grieghallen**, Bergen's glamorous concert hall, headquarters for the international festival of music, ballet and drama. In summer there are tours of the building—the last word in lighting and acoustical engineering.

Nearby Points of Interest

Gamle Bergen (Old Bergen), on the northern edge of town, shows yet again Bergen's fascination with its past. When significant 18th- and 19th-century houses in the city centre were condemned to make way for modern developments, they were not just torn down; instead they were moved to this outdoor museum. Well-informed guides take visitors inside typical houses, showing how rich and poor lived and worked. Note the strange antiques—moustache curlers, sewing machines, stoves, even an early Linotype machine in a fully equipped old print shop.

A reconstructed building of far greater age, **Fantoft Stavkirke** (Fantoft Stave Church), now stands at the top of a peaceful, wooded hill on the southern outskirts of Bergen. This typical Norwegian timber church was built in the 12th century in a village on the Sognefjord. In 1879 the parish decided to build a new church. People from Bergen saved the historic church from oblivion by buying the

Like stars, lights cascade from high ceiling in foyer of Grieghallen, *modern concert hall, with panorama of Bergen through picture windows.* 57

pieces and reassembling them here. It is still privately owned, and admission is charged to pay for the upkeep. There are countless details of interest in the ingenious design, with the ancient Viking ship shipbuilding techniques evident in the construction of the roof and the carvings of serpents and dragons as ornaments. (The church is a ten-minute walk from the bus stop in the immodestly named village of PARADIS.)

Troldhaugen (which means Troll Hill), a wooden house on a hilltop, was the home of composer Edvard Grieg (1843–1907). It's a 15-minute bus ride from Bergen to the hamlet of HOP, then a 20-minute walk through the countryside. Music lovers browse reverently amongst his scrawled manuscripts, photos and sketches. Grieg was a rare example of a composer appreciated during his lifetime—hence a room full of trophies, citations and honours, and a black Steinway he received as a present in 1892. Grieg bought Troldhaugen after he had composed his most famous lyrical works, the piano concerto and *Peer Gynt*. He continued working, sometimes in a small log cabin down at the waterfront. You can see how he left it, with notebooks on the work table and the scores of Beethoven's concertos lying on the chair and the upright piano. Grieg and his wife Nina, an opera singer, are buried at Troldhaugen, in a simple tomb in the side of a cliff.

Bergen Perspectives

Aside from the advertised attractions, Bergen lends itself to spontaneous strolls of discovery. You can't miss the grand old turreted firehouse, painted fire-engine red. Nearby, the bright former town hall, more than three centuries old, still stands on its dignity even though the administration has been transferred to a utilitarian mini-skyscraper. Small, old houses, once belonging to fishermen are set higgledy-piggledy in twisting cobbled streets. And something new always seems to be happening along the quays.

Sightseeing from the sea makes good sense. Excursions leave from the pier near the fish market; short tours cover the harbour, four-hour trips go into nearby fjords.

Seeing the port from the sea changes the outlook. Photographers can't resist taking pictures of the romantic three-masted sailing ship against the backdrop of the Hanseatic buildings. (The *Statsråd Lehmkuhl*, a training ship built in 1914, is open for visits.) The sailor's-eye view of the Bergenhus fortress shows its military advantages. Notice too the steep and stern-looking mountains just behind the heart of old Bergen.

Beyond the quay where the international ferries dock, another side of Bergen is revealed: the big modern fish factory, peeling old wooden warehouses and wharves, a refinery built to distill whale oil and now processing herring oil, a seaplane base for anglers' pleasure jaunts and rescue flights. You can also watch coastal express steamers docking in the next bay.

Across the water the big island of Askøy blocks any view of the open sea. Home of thousands of Bergen ferry commuters, Askøy is locally renowned for its strawberries.

Then round to the south harbour, with much more quay space than port. One melancholy sight: the one-time headquarters of German North Sea submarines. Three of the World War II U-boat berths sinisterly survive. The peacetime coastline more constructively is given over to a sprawling shipbuilding and repair industry.

You'll see old tramp steamers getting a facelift in drydocks, new freighters under construction, and perhaps an oil-drilling platform being refitted.

Bergen is one of those cities claiming seven hills (you can count them from the sightseeing boat). Two of these vantage points can be reached by Swiss-made mountain transport systems.

The swaying cable car to **Mt. Ulriken** (altitude almost 2,000 feet) is not only an exciting trip but a revealing survey of the geography of western Norway. You'll understand better why Bergen has thrived over many centuries, when you see how it's protected from the winds and tides by mountains, hills and interlocking fences of islands.

Fløybanen, the funicular from the centre of town to **Mt. Fløyen**, climbs a track at an incline of 26 degrees, with stops along the way for commuters. At the top—altitude 1,050 feet—there are hiking trails through the forest. Less energetic visitors can sit down to take in the view, or have a picnic in the pure, fresh air. And almost everybody tries for the perfect snapshot of the ships in the port and the red tile roofs and church spires of Bergen far below.

Norway in a Nutshell

For a whirlwind tour of some of Norway's most enthralling scenery, sign up for the train-boat-and-bus excursion called "Norway in a Nutshell". Even if you don't like package tours, you'll approve of this 12-hour short-cut to the world of fjords and waterfalls, mountains and magic valleys. Norwegian State Railways have had the wit to devise the itinerary, sell a master ticket, and then treat its customers like adults. You have to make your own connections, according to the timetable, and read your own map.

The morning leg of the trip is a train journey from Bergen, less than three hours, covering the western third of the Bergen Railway to Oslo. After the first half hour, you begin to see the charm of the little-publicized fjord, Sørfjorden, which parallels the track. Heading toward the mountainous centre of Norway, the vegetation changes to pine and spruce and delicately coloured wild flowers. Each railway station announces its altitude above sea level (*Høgd over havet*) in metres. Snow is seen on distant peaks and the lakes look too chilly for comfort. A narrow valley follows a river that changes its mood, from placid to raging, with every curve. Water-

falls of all kinds drip, spray, gush, bounce or roar down the steep hillsides. As the track rises above the tree line, the plateau looks green yet desolate. Snow-shelters, barriers and tunnels are a reminder that this lifeline stays open year-round only at great effort and expense.

At the junction village of MYRDAL, squashed between hills at an altitude of 2,844 feet, half the passengers stay aboard for Oslo or intermediate main-line points while the tourists disembark for the next stage of the nutshell.

River bisects an isolated hamlet in rugged mountain zone near Flåm.

After a short stop here, the Myrdal station-master, his uni-form like the captain of an ocean liner, sees off the little train to Flåm. *Flåmsbanen* (the Flåm line) 61 squeezes all the thrills of railroading into 12 miles and less than one hour of travel through sublime scenery from icy peaks to fjords. Downhill the trip takes 53 minutes, uphill 40 minutes. (Braking is the problem on the downward stretch, for the gradient is 1 in 18.)

Leaving Myrdal station, the line descends sharply through tunnels and snow-shelters. Once in the open, there are great panoramas of the wild green Flåm valley. Passing the mighty **Kjosfoss**, a waterfall whose spray covers the train with its fine mist, a photo stop is announced and passengers go out for a wet-lensed close-up.

Off to the left you see the incredibly zigzagging road which, until the Flåm line was opened in 1940, linked the valley with the Oslo-Bergen railway at the top. The old dirt road has 21 hairpin bends. As for the Flåm train, it follows its own zigzag, corkscrew course, so there are startling views of the next tunnel, or the next several tunnels, farther down the hillside. And all along the route the waterfalls outdo each other in size or beauty.

The track doesn't level out until it arrives at the terminal in FLÅM, a village huddling between an intimidating stone precipice and the fjord. Flåm is one of those places where all the day's excitement bubbles up at the arrival of the train, the bus and the ferry, all within a few steps of each other.

The schedule decrees a two-hour layover in Flåm, neatly timed for lunch and a bit of sightseeing around the head of the fjord. A fjord steamer, the next form of transportation, carries on along two arms of the Sognefjord through stirring scenery. Before going aboard, be sure to take a free map at the Flåm tourist office, showing all the points of interest along the route.

The fjord starting at Flåm is called the **Aurlandsfjord**, and the district's principal village, AURLAND, is the boat's first, brief stop. Aurland is noted for its Gothic stone church, built around 1200. The hamlet of UNDREDAL, farther along on the opposite bank, claims to have the smallest church in Norway—capacity 40 souls. Just up the way you can see farms perched high on the mountainsides on either side of the fjord, their land seemingly more suitable for eagles than farmers.

In the mountains at Bulken, near Voss: an old skill and an old mill.

A couple-of-minutes' journey from here the Aurlandsfjord joins the mainstream of the great Sognefjord (which goes all the way from here to the sea). But the boat turns off into another side channel, the **Nærøyfjord**. Here the scenery begins to take on the grandeur of a Grand Canyon setting. Mountain walls, and waterfalls, plunge into the narrow fjord. Sea birds nest in the crags, goats occupy tenuous clumps of grass, and along the waterline seals congregate. Seagulls, fluttering close enough to eat out of the hands of the passengers, follow the steamer to its last stop, the village of GUD-VANGEN.

From Gudvangen a scheduled bus service leads back up into the mountains. The trip begins with the climb up the steepest main road in the country, with 13 hairpin bends and ever more stupendous views of the fjord, the valley and the **Stalheimfoss**, which drops 413 feet in one mad rush. The drive on the narrow, twisting road, with a gradient up to 1 in 5, is so gruelling that tourists are moved to applaud the driver at the summit. Here a rest stop and photo session breaks the journey; the transients roam enviously through the Stalheim Hotell, a traditional resort hotel with overpowering **views** out over a precipice and up to the "sugarloaf" summit of Jordalsnuten.

More mountain roads and lakes and waterfalls follow, and the bus reaches Voss (see p. 46) in plenty of time for a coffee break before the train leaves for Bergen. Many

For the fearless, a stunning view over Lysefjord, near Stavanger.

64

a traveller who has over-indulged in scenic marvels keeps only half an eye on the country from Voss to the sea, for this part of the itinerary simply reverses the first couple of hours of the morning route.

The "Norway in a Nutshell tour" also allows you to add your own tangents to the circle. You can break the voyage anywhere and stop for the night—or a couple of months—pursuing any detours you like.

The Western Fjords

More than a century ago, the earliest tourists to Norway were astonished and captivated by the western fjords. Nothing much has changed since then except for a few pockets of industry taking advantage of the hydroelectric power generated by the waterfalls. The fjords are still a most inspiring sight. A compromise between mountains and sea, with thrilling vistas from above or below—even

Seaplane provides quick fjord-to-fjord connections and stupendous views down onto nearby glaciers.

if it does rain more often than absolutely necessary.

Vestlandet, the western fjord country, runs all the way from Stavanger in the south to the big-time fishing port of Kristiansund in the north. The fjords penetrate as far as 100 miles from the sea into the middle of the mountains, taking the form of stately bays or undulating streams or narrow channels imprisoned between cliff-faces.

Our brief survey covers only the most-visited parts of the most famous fjords, starting with the Hardangerfjord, east of Bergen, and then moving northward. Each fjord has its own character, mood and essential attractions. Don't try to see too much too fast. Even though today's travellers have the benefit of comfortable modern ferries and serviceable if narrow roads, the tranquil fjord country deserves to be experienced at a pensive pace. Besides, even if you get there in a hurry, you will only have to wait for the next ferry.

The Hardangerfjord

Partisans of the Hardangerfjord believe it's the most romantic of all. It certainly has something of everything—waterfalls and glaciers, orchards and pastures, and resort towns with all an escapist could want.

From Bergen to the heart of the fjord, highway E 68 is the most direct route—not to be confused with a straight road, which is a rarity in western Norway. The E 68 passes through the most varied scenery, from patches of suburbia to utter wilderness. After a full ration of mountain twists and turns, the final descent to the fjord reveals a majestic green valley. Just before you reach the town of Norheimsund, you pass the **Steinsdalsfoss**, a spectacular waterfall in a superb natural setting. A footpath goes up and under the roaring falls, so you can have a peek at this phenomenon while staying dry. NORHEIMSUND is a village where you can buy a bathing suit, snorkel and mask if the fjord suddenly looks inviting.

Another way to visit the Hardangerfjord is to take the popular do-it-yourself package tour in the "Nutshell" mould. It uses public transport (a comfortable bus that stops in the most remote places for country passengers) from Bergen to Norheimsund. Then comes a relaxing steamer voyage deep into the eastern wanderings of the Hardangerfjord. Mysterious islands loom in midstream, bare but for a few trees, a cottage or two and a rowboat. Some of the hillsides are crazily tilted; distant snow-speckled mountains, the forests below them, and the farmhouses in the foreground all seem packed together as if seen through a telephoto lens.

At the intersection of four arms of the fjord, the village of UTNE lies in the shadow of a steep hill with an unusual waterfall making a lateral detour in mid-drop. Utne is the site of the Hardanger Folk Museum.

KINSARVIK, across the fjord, has a Norman-style church built in the 12th century and the remains of a Viking boat-house. The hillsides here are *only* 45 degrees steep, which is almost flat for this part of the world.

LOFTHUS is as far south as the excursion steamer goes. Seaplanes and pleasure boats are parked in the fjord beside a modern luxury hotel, the visitors taking the afternoon sun right on the quayside. Edvard Grieg wrote some of his compositions in a garden next to **67**

WESTERN FJORDS

the hotel; other artists also found inspiration gazing across the fjord into the stark snowy mountain-side. Grieg got ideas from the hiss and roar of waterfalls and even the noise of mischievous boys rattling sticks down the length of the picket fence around his chalet.

From the quiet village of ULVIK, the view back down the narrow fjord shows ranks of hillsides projecting from left and right, overlapping in midstream to form a maze.

A tunnel west of the ferry port of BRURAVIK shortcuts the old road rounding the top of the fjord through Ulvik. Buses go to Voss through orchards and forests rising to an altitude where snowploughs are kept ready. Much of the trip on the switchbacked mountain road goes past, over and around photogenic waterfalls. The bus drivers, most considerate of the needs of camera-equipped tourists, even volunteer to stop where the best pictures can be snapped.

At Voss the bus connects with the train to Bergen. If you're driving yourself, you might prefer to pursue the Hardangerfjord farther south and west before returning to the seacoast. One idea: Go south from Lofthus down the ever-narrower Sørfjord to the industrial centre of ODDA, the base for excursions to a major glacier. The **Folgefonn** is its name, and you can walk to the edge from the place where the road runs out at BUAR. Don't get too close without a competent local guide, for snow-covered crevices can cause fatal surprises. But the Folgefonn diversion summarizes the wondrous Hardangerfjord; from apple blossoms to glacial ice within an hour's drive of each other.

The colours of Norway: ice-blue glacier, red barn, green orchard.

The Sognefjord

A foretaste of the Sognefjord was a highlight of the "Norway in a Nutshell" expedition. Veterans will remember a boat trip on the two southernmost extensions, the Aurlandsfjord and the Nærøyfjord. But there's much more to see on the Sognefjord, Norway's longest fjord: glaciers, waterfalls, cliff-faces striped like layer cake, inlets so quiet you can hear the fishermen in the next hamlet swapping tall stories. And on the steep hillsides the valiant farms look askew, like naïve paintings with the perspective all wrong.

You can drive there through Voss and Vangsnes. Or due north from Bergen, by several relaxing ferry hops, until you reach the seaward end of the fjord at the ferry terminals of Rutledal or Brekke. You then drive east along the little known north side of the fjord, sometimes only a few feet above the water, then climbing for unexpected new vistas of the fjord and fields far below. Until a new road conquers the mountains south-east of Høyanger, you'll have to take a ferry break from Nordeide to Kongsnes. From there it's an easy drive to the traditional resort of Balestrand.

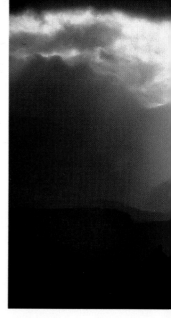

A different way to approach the Sognefjord is by express hydrofoil from Bergen. These big, sleek ships, fitted out with airliner seats, do the 98 nautical miles from Bergen to Balestrand in only four hours. Slower boats ply the same route, permitting more visibility and possibly a smoother ride. The sea trip north from Bergen, though protected by rows of islands and islets, may have a rough patch

Swooping in from the sea, a gull penetrates deep into fjord country.

or two before turning into the Sognefjord.

The Sognefjord tourist centre of BALESTRAND looks a bit like a tiny Swiss lake resort—minus the sidewalk cafés. Steamers and ferries call often enough to keep the quayside sunbathers awake. Balestrand is thought to have been inhabited some 5,000 years ago. By that standard the Viking burial mounds on the western outskirts of the village seem almost modern.

A popular excursion from Balestrand is the boat trip 13 nautical miles up the **Fjærlandsfjord,** a very narrow and idyllic offshoot of the Sognefjord. From the enticing resort village of FJÆRLAND, tourists go on by bus to the edge of

Norway's largest glacier, the Jostedalsbre. Fjærland is one of half a dozen villages on the periphery of this awesome empire of ice in which guides may be hired for expeditions across the glacier.

Back to Balestrand, which commands a crucial intersection in the fjord network. From here it's a short ferry jaunt to Vangsnes, across the busy shipping lanes. Like Balestrand, Vangsnes was a favourite holiday spot of Kaiser Wilhelm II. You can credit, or blame, the Kaiser for the gargantuan statue of Fridtjov the Valiant, an old Norse hero, on a hilltop above the poor defenceless town. Not many villages, in fact, would appreciate having overhead a sculpture 39 feet tall on a 47-foot granite base.

Several miles south of Vangsnes, the village of VIK (meaning cove or inlet) is known for its medieval churches. By far the most important is the **Hopperstad Stavkirke** (stave church), west of the town on a pleasant grassy knoll. This tall, elegant wooden church was built in the middle of the 12th century. Inside,

Hopperstad stave church, one of Norway's great achievements in architecture of the middle ages.

Frozen Powerhoses

A glacier is a moving sight, literally: a mass of ice, surviving year after year, slowly advancing or retreating (according to climatic conditions) along the mountain valleys.

You can sense the fearsome power even if a glacier doesn't look its best during the tourist season. Deprived of fresh snow, it's a bit grimy. But areas freshly exposed by avalanches are blinding white. And the fissures really are "ice blue".

For the last 10,000 years of temperate climate, it's been all downhill for glaciers. But Norway still counts more than 1,600 of the freezing flows, covering more than one per cent of the country's total area. It's still not too late to revisit the Ice Age.

---

some of the original Gothic sculptures and decorations have been preserved.

If you browse through a book of ferryboat schedules, you'll find that some of the timetables mention a stop in the Sognefjord called Midtfjords. The footnotes (in Norwegian only) explain that passengers from Balestrand to Gudvangen, for example, should make connections at Midtfjords. Midtfjords is simply the middle of the fjord, the local equivalent of the high seas. Boats from intersecting routes arrange to rendez-vous and passengers transfer from one boat to another. Cars, though, can't participate in this added adventure of the Sognefjord.

The Nordfjord

The Nordfjord thrusts nearly 60 miles inland, and it's the innermost area which offers the mildest climate and the most eye-catching scenery: craggy hills, lush meadows, waterfalls, turquoise lakes, and water reflecting the sky. There's also another chance to see Norway's biggest glacier.

If you arrive from the south on the road from BYRKJELO to UTVIK, your first view of the Nordfjord could hardly be more dramatic. On the final over-the-top stretch of the zigzagging road, the fjord suddenly appears and on the opposite bank the severe cliffs somehow seem upside down. At "normal" fjords, the little farms hug the shoreline, with cliffs rising behind them. But here the mountains fall almost vertically into the fjord; the pioneers have tacked their farms onto the cliff-top, dizzyingly close to the precipice.

Another curiosity of the inner Nordfjord: each of its three principal villages—Olden, Loen and Stryn—has its own lake. Yet another lake in the region, Hornindalsvatnet, claims the title of Europe's deepest lake (1,686 feet). It's so vast and sinuous that it might be mistaken for a fjord. Trout up to 22 pounds have been hooked in Hornindalsvatnet, but as in the lesser lakes, don't try it without a licence.

The resort village of **Olden,** spread out between the fjord and Olden's own substantial lake, is a good base for excursions to the glacier, **Jostedalsbreen**. Lake boats and buses provide alternatives to drive-it-yourself tours. From the end of the road 14 miles from Olden, it's about a 40-minute walk, mostly uphill, to the snow dunes. Another way up is by pony cart: the local Fjording ponies are sturdy and docile. However you go, be sure to wear comfortable shoes, for the last 10 minutes of the journey you will be using a path unfit even for pony carts. This leads to a pool a polar bear would love; mini-icebergs protrude in summer. Above, filling the head of the valley, the glacier itself emits a sense of overwhelming force. Only the foolhardy go unguided beyond the warning signs and onto the ice.

This finger of Jostedalsbreen is called Briksdalsbreen. Another offshoot, called Kjenndalsbreen, is reached through the village of LOEN, farther along the fjord. The road from Loen toward the glacier runs 13 miles to the south-east, almost always alongside Lake Loen. In 1905 a landslide of doomsday proportions created a tidal wave in Lake Loen, destroying villages and taking 61 lives. A repeat disaster in 1936 killed 74 people. From the point where the road runs out it's a half-hour walk to the glacier.

The Geirangerfjord

From the Nordfjord to the paragon of fjords, the Geirangerfjord, is an easy morning's drive. A roundabout but invigorating alternate route—still a morning's drive—turns east at the busy junction town of STRYN to follow the greatly improved Route 15 toward GROTLI. This rises above the treeline, with frosty lakes and plenty of snow patches in view. Route 58 to Geiranger branches off just after an especially enterprising tunnel. Route 58 is the widened version of a road nearly a century old—a zigzagging thriller. At an altitude above 3,300 feet, midsummer ice floes convene near the edge of the blue lake called Djupvatnet. Every summer, at the end of June there's an international ski competition held here.

A privately operated toll road, well-engineered but unpaved, encourages an exciting little side-trip up **Mount Dalsnibba** (about 5,000 feet). Unless the clouds have coasted in to blot out the view below, you won't begrudge the toll collector his steep fee for this transcendant scene of mountains, glaciers, lakes and the fjord itself.

Most maps can't fit in enough lines to indicate the true state of Highway 58 from Djupvatnet to the town of **Geiranger**. Measure the map and it's only four or five miles; drive the devious course and it's over ten. Even professional bus drivers look nervous on these tight, steep bends.

A big **lookout point** with parking space for cars and buses is built into the side of the descending road, and everybody's camera is clicking away at the scene a million posters and postcards have made the symbol of Norway. There's probably no new way to photograph this stunning scene from the safety of the railing at the Flydalsjuv, an outcrop of the cliff face arching over an abyss that

77

would be merely terrifying if the background weren't as heart-warming as any sight in the world. Below, the rapids cut through forests, verdant fields and a peaceful village on the edge of the fjord, which curves away between rugged hills laced with waterfalls and crowned with snow. You may forget the name "Geirangerfjord", but never this vista.

From on high the village seems no more than a few farmhouses strewn across a crescent of pasture. But Geiranger is bigger than it looks, with four modern hotels, plus motels and chalets to accommodate several times as many visitors as its own permanent population. One of the excitements here is the arrival of the big passenger ships, almost a daily happening. The view from Geiranger and nearby vantage points explains why this is the fjord most visited by the cruise-liners from near and far.

Many **waterfalls** enter the fjord and the highest, widest and most unusual ones have names of their own: among them are De Syv Søstre (The Seven Sisters) and the brooding Friaren (The Suitor—because it looks as if it's proposing to the sisters). Shipboard guides announce the names, recount the legends, and point out the small, isolated farms perched along the sheer hillsides. Audacious or perhaps desperate settlers built their houses and barns into niches so high and perilously inclined that children and livestock had to be tethered. (Most of the farms have been abandoned in modern times.)

One of the hikes suggested by the Geiranger tourist office is an adventurous trek up ancient trails

Cruise ship visits Geirangerfjord, climax of many tourist itineraries.

to Skageflå, an abandoned farm. Here you can see Friaren at close hand. The fjord is 886 feet below the old homestead.

More precipitous agriculture can be seen on the aptly named Eagle's Road as it leaves Geiranger on the way north to the ferry port of Eidsdal. The road passes old farm buildings as it strains up the mountainside to an altitude of 2,050 feet.

Travellers taking the car ferry from Geiranger to HELLESYLT (one hour) are in for more thrills on the road north, toward STRANDA. Leaving Hellesylt the well-built highway climbs the sheer side of the fjord, with ever more breathtaking **views**. Near the top it's astounding to come across a "cattle crossing" warning sign and farm buildings virtually teetering on the edge of the cliff.

From Stranda a good highway makes easy going of the trip northwest to Norway's biggest fishing port, ÅLESUND. The colourful harbour juts deep into the centre of the town like a canal. From Ålesund you can fly to Bergen or Oslo—the airport, on a flat farming island at sea, can be reached by a tunnel road.

Or you can continue north by ship, into the authentic land of the midnight sun. Every day of the year the Coastal Express dauntlessly maintains Norway's lifeline to the arctic.

Far beyond Arctic Circle, Coastal Express ship stops at Øksfjord.

Coastal Express

The world's most experienced, sophisticated travellers—people who casually compare notes on the pyramids of Egypt and Mexico, the straits of Gibraltar and Magellan—rave about *Hurtigruten* (the Coastal Express).

Every night a steamer leaves Bergen (you can pick it up in Ålesund the next afternoon) for the very far north: half the route lies within the Arctic Circle. The whole round-trip, from Bergen to the Norwegian mining town of Kirkenes on the Soviet border and back again, takes 11 days—about 2,500 miles

COASTAL
EXPRESS

Nordkapp
Kirkenes
Hammerfest
Lakselv
Alta
0   100 km
0   100 miles
Tromsø
Harstad
Hinnøy   Narvik
S
Sulitjelma   Arctic Circle
Bodø   1913
W
Hestmannøy   E
Polarsirkelen   Mosjøen   D
Kvigtind   E
1703
Rørvik   N
Namsos
Steinkjer
Trondheim
Kristiansund   Røros
Molde   2286
2138   Z
Ålesund   Glittertind
2452
Florø   Hamar
OSLO
Drammen
Bergen   Nupseggi   Sandefjord
1674
Fredrikstad
Haugesund   Arendal
Stavanger   Skagerrak
N
O
R
T
H

S
E
A
Kristiansand

of uncommon adventure in comfort.

Not that the Coastal Express pretends to be a luxury cruise. Forget about dancing, roulette tables and duty-free drinks. These are essentially workhorse cargo ships on which the tourists take second place to the national goal of keeping the northern towns of Norway linked and supplied all year in all weather. So even the first-class cabins are rather spartan. Nevertheless, *Hurtigruten* is so coveted that travel agents recommend booking a year in advance to be sure of convenient dates.

The sights from shipboard—glaciers, jagged mountains, lighthouses, coastal hamlets, islands of all kinds—continue to fascinate day after day. Add the midnight sun, the sea birds and the intoxication of sea air, and you'll realize that this is one of the world's unique travel experiences. Every few hours the ship pulls into a port, perhaps so small that only the local postmaster accepts the mail sack, the children come out to wave and the ship is on its way again. At important towns, cargo-loading commitments give the passengers time to disembark and pursue landward excursions.

A few highlights, south to north:

Arctic salmon fishing at Neiden near Soviet and Finnish borders.

Molde. "Town of Roses", founded officially in 1742, bombed in 1940, cheerfully rebuilt with gardens everywhere—even on the roof of the new city hall.

Kristiansund. Picturesque fishing town, fetchingly rebuilt after wartime devastation. The new Kirkelandet kirke (church), is by the Oslo architect Odd Østbye.

Offshore: the 82 islands comprising the municipality of Grip, with storm-battered cottages bunched around a red-painted stave church partially rebuilt in the 15th century.

Trondheim. Norway's medieval ecclesiastical and cultural centre, now the third biggest city in the country. Proudest landmark: **83**

Nidarosdomen (Cathedral of Nidaros), a monumental Gothic cathedral built in the 12th and 13th centuries, with a statue-studded façade and properly regal interior, all assiduously restored. Elsewhere in this roomy fjord-side city of parks and flowers, **Stiftsgården**, an immense wooden rococo mansion of the late 18th century, deserves a visit—though it's closed when in use as a royal residence. Out of town, the **Museum of Musical History** at Ringve preserves locks of hair of Liszt and Wagner and the world's smallest playable violin, no bigger than a postage stamp.

Rørvik. A village guarding the Nordland channel, a legendary battleground of giants and trolls. This is also around the place where mapmakers usually snip Norway in two to make the long skinny pieces fit onto a page.

Arctic Circle. Diplomas are distributed to passengers crossing this invisible but evocative line,

which passes through the island of Hestmannøy.

Bodø. In spite of the harsh latitude, this is a busy and agreeable town of more than 30,000, totally reconstructed since the German bombing of 1940 destroyed most of the buildings including the cathedral. The postwar cathedral, dedicated in 1956, is considered a triumph of modern architecture.

North of Bodø the ship crosses the open Vestfjord (smooth sailing cannot be guaranteed) with a distant view of islands and rocks inhabited by millions of sea birds. Seaward you can see the volcanic and granite peaks of "The Lofot Wall", a 60-mile-long chain of mountains on islands of the Lofoten group.

Harstad. An important fishing and military town on Norway's biggest island, Hinnøy, known for its 13th-century fortress church, Trondenes kirke, just a short way from the waterfront.

Tromsø. This bustling town has been called the "Paris of the North" and "Gateway to the Arctic". It's the home of the world's northernmost university, not to

A land for hardy folk: Lofoten islands' fishing boats in harbour; mountain climber stands by tent.

mention the world's northernmost brewery and pub. Coastal Express ships stop long enough for visits to the Tromsø Museum, specializing in arctic phenomena and Sámi folklore, or the cable car reaching Storsteinen, nearly 1,400 feet above the town and the sea. **85**

Hammerfest. At latitude 70° 39' 48", Hammerfest proudly proclaims itself the world's northernmost town. During the midnight sun season, this is a delightful distinction, but the inhabitants see no sun at all for two months of the long winter. Fishing and fish processing are mainstays of the economy.

Nordkapp (North Cape). King Oscar II paid a visit here in 1873, so this imposing cliff 1,007 feet above the sea can't be all that inaccessible. Actually, Coastal Express tourists nowadays get there by bus through Lapp and reindeer country.

Kirkenes. The exotic iron-mining town offers guided tours of the facilities. Passengers can take an excursion to the Soviet border, only a ten-minute drive from the quay, for a peek into the top corner of Eastern Europe.

Once a week in high summer a supplementary sailing undertakes the bold voyage to **Spitzbergen**, the Norwegian island on the edge of the polar ice-cap.

An alternative to the six-day return trip would be to take the bus and railway via the inland route. This will give you an opportunity to see more of the Sámi culture.

What to Do

Sports

For the Norwegians, active sports are an addiction. A weekend deprived of skiing, skating, sailing or fishing feels empty. They've even built chapels next to the ski runs to preclude any conflict of interest on a Sunday morning.

Skiing, invented in Norway, dominates the winter scene. From the king to kindergarten children, everyone hits the trail for cross-country skiing from November to May. Since this includes the darkest time of year, lights have been installed on dozens of ski paths around Oslo. They extend for more than 60 miles.

Apart from cross-country skiing, downhill is also popular. All the leading ski resorts have tows and lifts. Insatiable skiers can keep on going right into the summer at resorts along the glaciers.

Cross-country skiers travel through wilderness snowscape in the far north. This is virtually a universal sport in Norway, birthplace of skiing.

Summer Sports

In summer, activities offer as much variety as the country itself, from rock climbing to scuba diving.

Fishing is a logical favourite in a country with thousands of miles of coastline and hundreds of thousands of lakes and rivers, where the salmon and sea-trout are legion and any child can catch a bucket full of pike and perch. The locals pop into a rowboat, pull over to a favourite spot and toss out a line, confident that the fish have been waiting for this moment. The situation is somewhat more complicated on inland waterways, where a national fishing licence is required, plus local permits. Sea fishing for sport entails no paper-work, but there are restrictions in certain seasons. The best course is to study the pamphlet *Angling in Norway*, available from Norwegian tourist offices, and then make enquiries about particular conditions on the spot.

Boating and sailing. Most hotels and camping sites situated on lakes or fjords rent or lend boats to their guests. Elsewhere, many towns have facilities for renting rowing boats, canoes, sailing dinghies or motorboats. Serious sailors will find great sport in Norway, with the coast sheltered by thousands of islands and skerries and no shortage of welcoming harbours. Bookstores stock all the necessary navigation charts.

Swimming. Water temperatures in the Oslo Fjord often exceed 20°C (68°F) in summer, so those swimmers you see are neither polar bears nor masochists. The secret ingredient is the Gulf Stream, which makes the southern fjords swimmable from June to the beginning of September. Beaches are rather rare, but the locals enjoy sunbathing and swimming off the rocks. Heated indoor and outdoor pools are found in many towns.

Water-skiing is a feature of the leading resort hotels, which have boats and equipment for rent and in some cases instructors on duty.

Mountain climbing, a very popular activity in Norway, is highly organized, with marked

trails, excellent maps, and conveniently positioned chalets or huts. Courses are given in rock and glacier climbing. All information from the Norwegian Touring Association: Den Norske Turistforening (DNT) Stortingsgaten 28, Oslo 1.

Hiking and **rambling** are so much a part of the Norwegian way of life that the law guarantees everyone the right to cross private property (providing it's uncultivated). In fact, the Norwegian language has no word for "trespass". However, some restrictions are imposed. For instance, while pick-

Young enthusiasts stride across the great outdoors; rambling and hiking attract millions of citizens.

ing flowers, mushrooms and berries is permitted, the beloved cloudberries may be gathered (by law) only when ripe.

Cycling. Outside the big towns, motor traffic is not much of a bother; some towns have set aside special cycling routes. Many hotels and tourist offices rent bikes by the day.

Tennis. Some resort hotels include tennis courts in the roster of attractions. Several mountain hotels run tournaments.

Golf. The season may be short, but you can squeeze in a lot of play during the sunlit hours of summer. The Trondheim Golf Club issues a "Midnight Certificate" to late-night golfers. There are other courses in Oslo and Bergen.

Horseback riding. Stables in Oslo and at some country hotels have horses and ponies for hire. Several riding centres organize horseback tours through the countryside for up to a week. Enquire at the tourist office.

Shopping

VAT, or sales tax, called "moms", is about 15 per cent on all products and services. This tax will be refunded in cash within four weeks of purchase at the point of departure to non-Scandinavian visitors who buy in shops displaying the red-white-and-blue "Tax free for Tourists" sticker (present your passport). You simply show the Tax-free Shopping Cheque provided by the shop (its back duly filled out by yourself) at the port, airport, ship or border. Note that you must not use the article prior to leaving Norway.

Den Norske Husflidsforening (The Norwegian Association for Home Arts and Crafts) has shops

Artisans at work: Sámi women create typical jewellery in village of Kautokeino; woodcarver (opposite) takes advantage of nature's quirks.

(called *Husfliden*) in most towns, offering the best of Norwegian arts and crafts.

Shops are normally open 9 a.m. to 5 p.m. Monday–Friday (till 7 p.m. on Thursdays), 9 a.m. to 1 p.m. on Saturdays.

Best buys

Here, alphabetically arranged, are some of the items to look for in department stores, boutiques or country artisans' shops.

Cardigans, mittens, scarves and ski-caps are hand-knitted or machine-made in typical Norwegian patterns. The most traditional of the sweaters is a jacket-like model called a *lusekofte*.

Carvings, painted wooden figurines of Norwegian characters—fishermen, milkmaids, sailors, skiers and Sámi (with reindeer to accompany them).

Cheese slicers, those handy Norwegian implements for producing paper-thin shavings of cheese —not, as some people imply, for stingy motives but because some cheeses taste better that way. Slicers and knives come in pewter, stainless steel or silver-plate, often with Norwegian designs.

Furs: Norwegian fox and mink pelts are highly esteemed, though not for all budgets or tastes.

Glassware and crystal: glasses, flasks, vases, plates and figurines. Many designs are both original and sophisticated.

Hunting knives and fishermen's knives in handy scabbards.

Miniature Viking ships of wood, pewter, enamel or silver, **91**

with or without sails. And the 1990s variation—models of oil-drilling platforms.

Pewter mugs, glasses, trays and drinking horns, usually with Viking or other traditional motifs in relief.

Pottery: although Norway's ceramicists have to import the clay to work from, they produce many articles in beautiful yet service-able country-style designs: coffee mugs, sugar bowls, plates and candle-holders, among others.

Rocks: glittering minerals from Norway's mountains, much ap-preciated by collectors.

"Rose-painted" wooden arti-cles, such as small boxes, egg cups, plates and miniature bel-lows: the painted rococo floral designs are typical Norwegian decorations.

Sporting goods: look for the latest designs in skiing, fishing, boating and camping equipment made by Norwegian firms for their demanding customers.

Trolls: small enough to pocket or tall as a table, whimsical like-nesses of these characters, looking half bear, half leprechaun, are so ubiquitous you may find it impossible to leave Norway with-out one of your own.

Woven goods: tapestry weav-ing has been an art in Norway since Viking times. There is a fine selection of woven runners, cloths and wall hangings to choose from. Be sure to look, too, at *ryer* rugs, tablecloths and napkins.

Festivals and Special Events

Check with local tourist offices so you don't miss out on any special celebrations. Norway's main events are:

March.	Holmenkollen, Oslo. Ski-jumping championship.
17 May.	Constitution Day. Parades in all the towns.
May–June.	Bergen International Festival (two weeks).
23 June.	Midsummer bonfires and folklore everywhere.
29 July.	Stiklestad. St. Olav Festival (Olsok).
August.	Molde. Jazz festival.
	Stavanger Sea Fishing Competition.

Folk dancers in authentic regional costumes perform in the sunshine.

Entertainment

Something's always going on in Oslo—until 4 a.m. in a few cases. Smaller towns have a reduced range of attractions, but unless you find yourself in a very sleepy village, the chances are you'll be offered some organized diversions. For details of shows, look in brochures like *Oslo This Week* and *Bergen This Week*.

Folklore shows. Old-time songs and village dances by performers in national costumes are regularly scheduled in Oslo and Bergen. In

Oslo they are staged in the bold modern Concert Hall and outdoors at the Norwegian Folk Museum. Bergen visitors may book an excursion to a simulated country wedding with traditional food, music and folk dancing (Fana Folklore).

Nightclubs. Oslo is unlikely to be confused with New York or Paris in the nightlife department, but nobody will be forced to go home early. Dancing and floor shows go on late in nightclubs and discos with live bands and recorded music. Cocktail bars (normally **93**

found in hotels only) and pubs close earlier, usually by midnight. In small towns and holiday resorts, the action is usually concentrated on the leading (or only) hotel, which may have a dance band in residence. Oslo also has several jazz clubs.

Theatre. During the height of the tourist season, the theatrical scene reaches low ebb, though a few Oslo theatres usually put on plays in English in summer. In Bergen you might have a chance to see a play in the theatre where Ibsen worked, Den Nationale Scene.

Concerts. Top concerts, operas and pop performances take place in Oslo's new Concert Hall and Bergen's glittering Grieg Hall. Organ recitals are often held in historic churches.

Cinemas. All films are shown with the original sound-track and Norwegian subtitles.

For Children. The kids will enjoy a day out at Norway's first **amusement park**, Tusen-Fryd, 12 miles outside Oslo on the E 18. Or you could take them to the *International Museum of Children's Art* (*Barnekunsthistorisk Museum*) at Lille Frøensv. 4 in Oslo. This one-of-a-kind institution displays the work of budding talents from around the world.

Eating in Norway

Some of the best food in Norway comes fresh from the sea, which is only natural in one of the world's leading fishing nations. You can surround yourself with luxury and dine on lobster or salmon. Or go down to the waterfront and pick up a picnic lunch of shrimp right off the boat*.

Meat-eaters have no need to feel abandoned either, for though Norway is floundering in seafood, there are original beef, pork, mutton and game dishes, too.

What's called a *restaurant* in Norway is a serious eating place where people go for a major meal. Many restaurants are licensed to serve wine and beer: the most elegant ones often have additional permission to serve spirits. Dress tends to be formal; some places require women to wear dresses and men to wear jackets in the evening.

A *kafé* or *kafeteria* is an informal, less expensive eating place, usually self-service, offering adequate but not elaborate meals. Some sell beer and wine.

---

* For a comprehensive guide to dining in Norway, consult the Berlitz EUROPEAN MENU READER

Specialities of the *konditori* are pastries served with coffee or tea, and usually sandwiches as well.

To encourage tourism, hundreds of restaurants offer a special cut-price menu in summer. Participating restaurants display the campaign's symbol, a gourmet bear marked "Feriemeny" ("holiday menu").

A service charge will always be included in the bill, so tipping is optional, but good service usually rates an extra 5 to 10 per cent.

Meal Times

Breakfast (*frokost*) is usually served between 8 and 10 a.m., lunch (*lunsj*) between 11 a.m. and 1 p.m., but sandwiches and snacks are available in a variety of eating places from mid-morning. Some hotels and restaurants put on a smørgåsbord-style lunch from around noon. Dinner (*middag*) is the main meal of the day for Norwegians, and is eaten in Norwegian homes any time between 2 and 7 p.m. The evening meal at hotels and big restaurants may start at about 7 p.m., much earlier in smaller establishments.

Breakfast

Country hotels and certain city hotels offer huge breakfasts in serve-yourself style: cheeses, cold

meats, herring, cole slaw, beets, cold cereal, breads and crispbreads, butter and jam, juice, milk, coffee or tea. But the trend seems to be away from these extravaganzas to the Continental breakfast.

Lunch and Dinner

Smørbrød means bread and butter, which is quite an understatement when you consider Scandinavia's reputation for elaborate open sandwiches. Almost anything may turn up on one of these appetizing *smørbrød:* roast beef (*roastbiff*), ham (*skinke*), sliced egg (*egg*), shrimp (*reker*), mayonnaise salads, like *italiensk salat* ("Italian" salad—sliced ham, cabbage, onion in mayonnaise), *rekesalat* (shrimp salad), *sildesalat* (herring salad).

Koldtbord

The Swedish name, smorgåsbord, is better known than its Norwegian equivalent, *koldtbord* (literally, cold table). Some restaurants and mountain hotels specialize in this bountiful self-service banquet. The rules guarantee that you can fill your plate as often as you like for the same price. But to be civilized, your first plate should deal with fish and seafood. Use a fresh plate for meat, salads and egg dishes. And another

for sweets. In between there are often several hot dishes, as well.

Norwegian Specialities

The most "national" food of all is what Norwegians call **spekemat** (cured food). Be sure to try *spekeskinke* (cured ham), *spekepølse* (cured sausage), *fenalår* (cured leg of mutton) and *fårepølse* (cured mutton sausage), which all have a long tradition in the country since curing was the only way of conserving food in the olden days. Usually the *spekemat* is served with crisp, paper-thin bread (*flatbrød*) and scrambled eggs. With this delicious food one drinks cold beer and *akevitt*.

A uniquely Norwegian dish is **rømmegrøt** (sour-cream porridge), which when served with sugar and cinnamon is tasty, refreshing and very filling.

Any country with winters like Norway's is bound to develop a hearty repertoire of **soups**. Vegetables feature in some of the favourites: *betasuppe* (a thick meat-and-vegetable soup), almost a dish in itself, and the very filling *gul ertesuppe* (yellow pea soup) laced with ham. *Fiskesuppe* (fish soup) is a rich brew made richer with egg yolks and cream.

Fish dishes are excellent in Norway. Among the tastiest, but

Appease your hunger at a Norwegian do-it-yourself buffet.

expensive, fish are salmon (*laks*), trout (*ørret*) and sea trout (*sjø-ørret*). Boiled cod with liver (*kokt torsk med lever*) is a particular delicacy, as is halibut (*hellefisk*).

Among Bergen specialities are *seibiff med løk* (fried coalfish with onions) and *avkokt pale og fiske-suppe* (boiled young coalfish with fish soup).

97

Fish as a starter enjoys wide popularity in Norway, including *sild* (herring)—served in a number of pickled or marinated forms. And no gourmet could ask for a more exquisite treat than *gravlaks* (cured salmon), served thinly sliced with a wedge of lemon, or with dill and mustard sauce. Another speciality for connoisseurs is *rakørret* (half-fermented trout)—but only the most daring foreign tourists will try it. *Hvalbiff* (whale steak) is tender and steak-like,

with no hint of the sea in its flavour.

Meat, popular in Norway since Viking times, still figures prominently in the Norwegian diet; for example, *lammekoteletter* (lamb chops) and *fårestek* (roast leg of mutton). *Fårikål* (lamb or mutton and cabbage stew) is a national tradition. The stew, together with black pepper and a little flour, is cooked in a big pot.

Kjøttkaker (meat balls), as popular as they are filling, are often

served with *surkål* (sweet-and-sour cabbage) or with *løk* (fried onions). *Lapskaus*, a tasty stew of chopped meat, potatoes, onion and other vegetables, is dished up brown (*brun*—with fried meat) or white (*lys*—with boiled meat). *Svineribbe* (spare-rib) is mainly eaten at Christmas.

Game and fowl are important variations on the menu, from roast chicken to *rugde* (woodcock) or *elg* (elk). *Rype i fløtesaus* (ptarmigan in cream sauce) and *reinsdyrstek* (roast reindeer thinly sliced) are served with boiled potatoes and cranberry sauce.

Desserts and Sweets

These often rely on whipped cream, which might make you wonder how the Norwegians keep so slim when they shamelessly pack away the very richest cakes. A conservative example might be *tilslørte bondepiker* (literally, "veiled farmgirls"), layers of stewed apples, biscuit crumbs, sugar and whipped cream. *Bløtkake* ("soft cake"), a sponge cake filled with fruit and whipped cream, is the most popular of all Norwegian cakes. Nobody would think of

Country-style goat's milk cheese takes shape on an old wood-stove.

celebrating a birthday without a *bløtkake* on the table. An even richer variant is the so-called *hvit dame* ("white lady") which has a covering layer of marzipan. Pancakes and waffles, too, are often served with cream and fruit preserves.

Norwegians go berserk over **berries**. They love to scour the countryside in search of wild berries, to eat them fresh and in jams. The supreme delicacy of this realm is *multer med krem* (arctic cloudberries with cream).

Cheese is eaten on *smørbrød*, rarely as a separate dish. Be sure to try one of the brown cheeses, of goat's milk (*geitost*) or mixed goat's and cow's milk (*gudbrandsdalsost* and *mysost*). If conventional cheeses are too bland for your taste, look for *gammelost* (old-fashioned cheese). In days of yore it was matured in straw in the barn; it still tastes that way. In addition to Norwegian cheeses like *ridderost* and *jarlsbergost*, there are fine local versions of Brie, Camembert and Roquefort.

Drinks

Norwegians often drink plain tap water with their meals. If you prefer mineral water, bubbly *farris* is refreshing. Soft drinks and excellent juices are also on sale.

Alcoholic beverages of any sort are subject to stringent regulations. Spirits are served at most major hotels and restaurants but only from 3 to 11 p.m. or midnight and never on Sunday or holy days; beer and wine are more widely available, Sundays included (from 12 noon), but by no means everywhere. To buy a bottle of wine or spirits you must go to one of the state-run shops (*Vinmonopol*), open during normal shopping hours, where the product is presented in a grimly antiseptic light; and the prices are discouraging, too.

Local beers meet international standards. *Pils* is the generic term for lager, *export* is stronger. If you're driving, stick to *brigg* or *zero*, beers which are virtually non-alcoholic. *Vørterøl* is a non-alcoholic dark and rather sweet "beer".

Wines are imported from many countries. As taxes are so high, wine is not the daily habit of more southerly climes.

Akevitt (aquavit), the local fire-water, is derived from potatoes or barley. Served ice-cold in tiny glasses with meals, it is usually washed down with beer. Delicious, but not to be tippled flippantly. *Skål!*

To Help You Order...

Could we have a table?	**Kan vi få et bord?**
I'd like to pay.	**Jeg vil gjerne betale**.
Keep the change.	**Behold resten**.

I'd like ...

Jeg vil gjerne ha ...

beer	**en øl**	milk	**melk**
bread	**brød**	mustard	**sennep**
butter	**smør**	potatoes	**poteter**
cheese	**ost**	rice	**ris**
coffee	**kaffe**	salad	**salat**
dessert	**en dessert**	sandwich	**et smørbrød**
fish	**fisk**	soup	**en suppe**
fruit	**frukt**	sugar	**sukker**
ice-cream	**en iskrem**	tea	**te**
lemon	**sitron**	(iced) water	**(is-)vann**
meat	**kjøtt**	wine	**vin**
menu	**spisekartet**	wine list	**vinkartet**

...and Read the Menu

agurk	cucumber	**kylling**	chicken
and	duck	**kål**	cabbage
ansjos	marinated sprats	**laks**	salmon
appelsin	orange	**lammekjøtt**	lamb
blomkål	cauliflower	**lapskaus**	meat stew
blåbær	bilberries/ blueberries	**lever**	liver
blåskjell	mussels	**lutefisk**	cured boiled stockfish
bringebær	raspberries	**løk**	onion
bønner	beans	**multer**	arctic cloud-berries
dyrestek	roast venison		
eggerøre	scrambled eggs	**oksekjøtt**	beef
eple	apple	**ost**	cheese
erter	peas	**poteter**	potatoes
fasan	pheasant	**pølser**	sausages
fenalår	cured leg of mutton	**reinsdyrstek**	roast reindeer
flyndrefilet	fillet of plaice/ flounder	**reker**	shrimp
		rype	ptarmigan
		sild	herring
fløte/krem	cream	**sjampinjonger**	button mush-rooms
fårekjøtt	mutton	**sjøtunge**	sole
grønnsaker	vegetables	**skinke**	ham
gulrøtter	carrots	**sopp**	mushrooms
gås	goose	**stekt**	fried
hellefisk	halibut	**surkål**	sweet-and-sour cabbage
hummer	lobster		
hvalbiff	whale steak	**svinekjøtt**	pork
hvitting	100whiting	**svisker**	prunes
jordbær	strawberries	**terte**	tart
kalkun	turkey	**torsk**	cod
kalvekjøtt	veal	**torskerogn**	cod roe
karbonadekake	hamburger steak	**tunfisk**	tunny/tuna
		tyttebær	cranberries/ lingonberries
kjeks	biscuits		
kjøttkaker/ kjøttboller	meat balls	**vafler**	waffles
		vaktel	quail
kokt	boiled, cooked	**ørret**	trout
kolje	haddock	**østers**	oysters
kreps	crayfish	**ål**	eel

BLUEPRINT for a Perfect Trip

How to Get There

Although the fares and conditions described below have all been carefully checked, it is advisable to consult a travel agent for the latest information on fares and other arrangements.

From North America

BY AIR: Non-stop flights depart daily from New York (Newark) for Oslo's Fornebu Airport. Daily connecting service is available from 30 North American centres, and on specific days of the week from another 40 cities in the U.S. and Canada.

Various reduced-price tickets, such as Pex, Apex, Super-Apex and Youth Pex are offered.

Charter Flights and Package Tours: Reduced rates are featured on tours to Norway in May and September. Group Inclusive Tours (GIT) are currently being offered for 2 to 18 days; the longer tours add visits to the other Scandinavian countries plus Russia and Poland. The GIT package covers airfare, accommodation, meals and sightseeing expenses.

Visitors from outside Europe may travel on the Eurailpass, a flat-rate unlimited-mileage ticket, valid for first-class rail travel anywhere in Western Europe outside Great Britain. Eurail Youthpass is similar to the Eurailpass, but offers second-class travel at a cheaper rate to anyone under 26.

From Great Britain

BY AIR: Several daily non-stop flights link London and Oslo. In addition, direct services operate to Oslo from Aberdeen, Manchester and Newcastle. Flying time is approximately 3 hours. There are also direct flights from Aberdeen, Glasgow, London and Newcastle to Bergen and Stavanger.

Fares available on these flights include Economy, Budget, Apex and Youth Fare.

Charter Flights and Package Tours: One package offered includes 4–7 nights in Oslo. Accommodation is available in "budget", "regular" and "superior" categories. Students and other economy-minded travellers will find the budget accommodation (a youth hostel) simple but very attractively priced.

BY SEA: You can sail from Newcastle to Bergen all year round.

BY RAIL: The Scandinavian Express travels from London to Copenhagen, where you change to a night express for Oslo. You can purchase a first-class or tourist-class ticket. Sleeping cars are available. Total travel time, London to Oslo is about 34 hours. See also page 122.

When to Go

The best time to visit Oslo, Bergen and the Norwegian mountains and fjords is from mid-spring to mid-autumn, when the days are long and the temperatures pleasant. Even for skiing, spring is the best time. There is likely to be less rain in May and June than in July.

The following chart will give you an idea of the average daily maximum and minimum temperatures in Oslo.

	J	F	M	A	M	J	J	A	S	O	N	D
Max.°F	28	31	39	50	61	68	72	69	61	49	38	32
°C	-2	-1	4	10	16	20	22	21	16	9	3	0
Min. °F	19	19	24	33	42	50	55	53	46	38	31	24
°C	-7	-7	-4	1	6	10	13	12	8	3	-1	-4

Planning Your Budget

Here are some average prices in Norwegian kroner (kr) for basic expenses. However, remember that all prices must be regarded as *approximate*.

Airport transfers. *Oslo*: taxi kr 130, coach kr 30. *Bergen*: taxi approx. kr 200, coach kr 36.

Camping (three-star site). Daily rate per car and tent or caravan (trailer) and passengers kr 110, plus kr 20 for electricity. Cabin (four beds) kr 390, kr 630 with shower/toilets.

Car hire. *Ford Fiesta* (3 dr.) kr 520 per day, kr 5.94 per km., kr 6,600 per week with unlimited mileage. *Ford Sierra* (3 dr.) kr 670 per day, kr 7.80 per km., kr 8,130 per week with unlimited mileage. *Volvo 240 Station Wagon* (5 dr.) kr 785 per day, kr 8.94 per km., kr 7,400 per week with unlimited mileage. VAT included.

Entertainment. *Cinema* kr 50, *theatre* kr 80–290, *nightclub* kr 50.

Hairdressers. *Woman's* haircut kr 200, shampoo and set or blow-dry kr 150, permanent wave kr 600. *Man's* haircut kr 150.

Hotels (double room with bath and breakfast). Expensive kr 1,600, medium kr 900, budget kr 500.

Meals and drinks (medium-priced restaurant). Lunch table kr 130, one-course lunch kr 85, dinner (entrecôte, à la carte) kr 130, *smørbrød* kr 50, glass of beer kr 28, soft drink (glass) kr 14, half a bottle of medium-priced wine kr 120, coffee kr 10.

Museums. Kr 5–30, sometimes free.

Supermarket. Loaf of bread kr 15, 250 g. of butter kr 9, six eggs kr 13, 1 kg. of rumpsteak kr 200, 1 kg. of hamburger meat kr 100, 250 g. of coffee kr 13, 200 g. of instant coffee kr 75, beer (small bottle) kr 12, soft drinks (small bottle) kr 7.

Transport. *City buses/trams*. Oslo: single ticket kr 13, card of 5 coupons kr 60, 12 coupons kr 135, 24-hour tourist ticket kr 40; Bergen: single ticket kr 6–11, 48-hour tourist ticket kr 45. *Taxi* meters start at kr 21 (short trips within city limits kr 40). *Train* Oslo–Bergen, one way first class kr 675, second class kr 450. *Coastal Express ship (Hurtigruten)* Bergen–Kirkenes–Bergen, meals included, kr 6,000–16,000 according to season and standard of comfort.

An A–Z Summary of Practical Information and Facts

An asterisk (*) following an entry indicate that relevant prices are to be found on page 105. Listed after many entries is the appropriate Norwegian translation, usually in the singular.

A

ACCOMMODATION*. See also CAMPING. Tourist office brochures list hotels *(hotell)* and boarding houses *(pensjonat/hospits)*, indicating category, number of beds, rooms (with or without bathroom or shower), and whether they are licensed to sell beer only, beer and wine, or are fully licensed, plus any garage facilities. Certain of these leaflets also give rates. Tourist offices can inform you about which hotels offer special low rates (either off-season or at weekends). Service charge is always included in the bill; usually breakfast is as well.

Oslo and Bergen hotels are often fully booked, so it's sensible to make reservations in advance. Write to:

Turistinformasjonen, Oslo S (the Central Railway Station), Jernbanetorget 1, 0154 Oslo 1; or: Turisttrafikkomiteens Informasjonssenter, Torgalmenningen, N-5000 Bergen

If you arrive in Oslo without a reservation, try the Tourist Information Centre at Rådhuset (City Hall).

In Bergen, the Tourist Information Office at Torgalmenningen assists in finding rooms during its regular office hours.

Youth hostels *(vandrerhjem)*. About 80 youth hostels are scattered throughout Norway, some of which are considered among Europe's best. No age limit is applied so that whole families travelling by car can take advantage of the economic accommodation—most useful in more remote districts. The majority of hostels require a membership card. If you aren't a member of the youth hostel association in your own country, you can obtain a guest card from the Norwegian Youth Hostels Association (branches in Oslo and Bergen):

Norske Vandrerhjem, Dronningens gt. 26, 0154 Oslo 1; tel. (02) 42 14 10

Norske Vandrerhjem, Strandgaten 4, 5013 Bergen; tel. (05) 32 68 80

Hostel in **Oslo**: *Haraldsheim Vandrerhjem*, Haraldsheimveien 4, 0587 Oslo 5; tel. (02) 22 29 65

In **Bergen**: *Montana Vandrerhjem*, Johan Blydtsvei 30; tel. (05) 29 29 00

AIRPORTS* *(flyplass/lufthavn)*. Oslo's airport, **Fornebu**, some 10 kilometres from the centre of town, is Norway's principal airport for international as well as domestic traffic. Services include a duty-free shop, a restaurant, a cafeteria, post office, bank (see MONEY MATTERS), telephone and telegraph facilities, car hire desks, news-stands and shops. Airport buses depart every 30 minutes for the Central Railway Station via the SAS city terminal and Hotel Scandinavia, Holbergs gt. 30.

Gardermoen airport, 53 kilometres north of Oslo, is used mainly for international charter traffic.

Bergen's airport is at **Flesland**, 19 kilometres south-west of the city. Though smaller than Fornebu, it boasts a duty-free shop, a restaurant, bank, post office, car hire desk, news-stand and several shops. Airport buses take passengers to Bergen city terminal (at the Central Bus Station), Strømsgt. 8 and continue from there to Hotel Norge and SAS Royal Hotel.

There are luggage trolleys at all airports, but no porters.

Domestic flights. When visiting Norway—in view of the long distances involved and, in certain cases, difficult road conditions—tourists may prefer to fly. Fifty airfields serve the country, some near towns difficult to get to; 20 of these take regular passenger flights, the routes being shared mainly between Braathens SAFE and SAS. The major airports are at Bodø, Kirkenes, Kristiansand, Stavanger, Tromsø, Trondheim and on Svalbard (Spitsbergen).

Ticket offices:

Oslo	Braathens SAFE, Haakon VII's gate 2; tel. (02) 59 70 00/83 44 70
	SAS, Ruseløkkveien 6; tel. (02) 83 77 60/59 62 40
Bergen	Braathens SAFE, Ole Bulls Pl. 4; tel. (05) 23 23 25
	SAS, Torgalmenningen 1; tel. (05) 23 63 30/23 63 00

BABY-SITTERS *(barnevakt)*. There is no organized baby-sitting service for tourists in Norway. However hotel receptionists or tourist offices will be of assistance in special situations. In Oslo, baby-sitting can be arranged through the National Employment Exchange Office *(Arbeidsformidlingens vikartjeneste)*, Trondheimsveien 2, tel. (02) 20 40 90.

C **CAMPING***. Campsites in Norway provide clean, comfortable, though spartan, accommodation amid beautiful scenery. There are more than 1,300 registered sites throughout the country, classified by one, two or three stars according to amenities. Though most campers live in tents, cabins have become increasingly popular, and rates are reasonable. The season is normally from mid-May or early June till the end of August.

Oslo   *Bogstad Camping*, 10 kilometres from city centre, three stars
        Ekeberg Camping, 4 kilometres from city centre, two stars
        Frognerstrand Camping, 60 kilometres north-east of Oslo, two stars
        Hersjøen Camping, 50 kilometres north of Oslo, three stars
        Stubljan Camping, 9 kilometres south of Oslo, two stars

Bergen   *Grimen Camping*, 15 kilometres south of Bergen, two stars
        Lone Camping, 20 kilometres south of Bergen, three stars
        Midttun Camping, 11 kilometres south of Bergen, two stars

CAR HIRE*. See also DRIVING. The major international car hire agencies as well as reliable local firms are represented in both Oslo and Bergen and at the cities' respective airports. Addresses figure in the classified telephone directory *(Gule Sider)* under "Bilutleie".

To hire a car, minimum age is 23, 25 or even 30, depending on the company and size of car. You'll need your driving licence and passport. A cash deposit is normally required, but this is waived if you present a major international credit card.

CIGARETTES, CIGARS, TOBACCO *(sigaretter, sigarer, tobakk)*. Virtually all international cigarette, cigar and tobacco brands are available in tobacco shops and kiosks. Local brands are quite good, and Norwegian pipe tobacco is noted for its quality.

Smoking here is a very expensive habit, however, and not popular with the authorities. Public advertising is banned. Smoking is forbidden in public places and in railway carriages marked "Røyking ulovlig". Even so, Norwegians are enthusiastic smokers.

A packet of …	**En pakke …**
filter-tipped/without filter	**med/uten filter**
A box of matches, please.	**En eske fyrstikker, er De snill.**

CLIMATE and CLOTHING. Thanks mainly to the influence of the Gulf Stream, Norway in fact enjoys a far more favourable climate than its northern latitude would make you think. Summers, for instance, are often warmer than in the U.K. Winters are long, but seldom impossibly cold (mean January temperature in Oslo is -5°C or 23°F, in Bergen 1.5°C or 35°F). Warm clothing is needed during late autumn, winter and early spring. Lightweight clothing generally suffices in summer, when the country (particularly in the north) hardly sees an hour of darkness. But even then, evenings tend to get chilly, so it is always a good idea to take along a jersey or wrap.

Bergen, capital of fjord-country, has the dubious privilege of being the most rained-upon town in Norway. When you're discovering the beauties of the fjords, you'll certainly appreciate having brought a raincoat with you, whatever the season.

Wherever you travel in Norway, comfortable walking shoes are essential.

Except for outings to theatres, concerts and better restaurants, Norwegians dress informally.

COMMUNICATIONS

Post offices (*postkontor*). Oslo's General Post Office, at Dronningens gt. 15 (Oslo 1), is open Monday–Friday from 8 a.m. to 8 p.m., until 3 p.m. on Saturdays.

Opening hours at most of Oslo's 100-odd other post offices are 8 a.m.–5.30 p.m., Monday–Friday (July 1–mid-August: 4.30 p.m.), and 9 a.m. to 1 p.m. on Saturdays.

Bergen's main post office at Rådstuplass 10 is open weekdays from 8 a.m. to 5 p.m. (until 7 p.m. on Thursdays), Saturdays from 9 a.m. to 1 p.m.

Stamps (*frimerke*) can also be bought at tobacco shops, kiosks and hotels. Postboxes are painted red.

Telephone (*telefon*), **telegram** and **telex** services are operated by the state Telecommunications Service, Televerket. At Kongens gt. 21 in Oslo, you can call, cable or telex from 8.30 a.m. to 9 p.m., and from 10 a.m. to 5 p.m. on Saturdays and Sundays.

Bergen's Central Telegraph and Telephone Building, Telegrafbygningen, by the City Park is open during the same hours as in Oslo.

Telephone booths are painted red or grey. Old ones are for local calls only; from new ones, local, long-distance and international calls can all be made. **109**

C For direct calls abroad, dial 095, then the country code, national trunk code and local telephone number. For operator assistance, see below.

Telegrams can be phoned in by dialling 0138.

Some useful numbers:

Operator for international calls	0115
Domestic and other Scandinavian enquiries	0180
Other international enquiries	0181

express (special delivery)	**ekspress**
registered	**rekommandert**
poste restante (general delivery)	**poste restante**
reverse-charge (collect) call	**noteringsoverføring**

CONVERTER CHARTS. For fluid and distance measures, see pp. 112 and 113. Norway uses the metric system.

Temperature

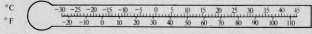

Length

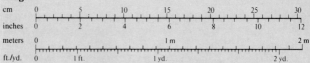

Weight

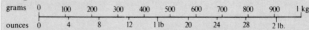

CRIME and THEFT. Both Oslo and Bergen, as cities elsewhere, have kept up with the times—which means that crime is on the increase. Cars—and their parts—are astronomically expensive, so they are the most likely objects of theft. Make sure valuables and belongings are locked up; simply take all elementary, common-sense precautions.

CUSTOMS (toll) **and ENTRY REGULATIONS**. See also DRIVING. Visitors from Great Britain can enter Norway with a Visitor's Passport. Visitors from the U.S.A., Canada, Eire, Australia and New Zealand need only a valid passport. Visitors from South Africa must have visas. You are entitled to stay in the country for up to three months without a visa.

The following chart shows what main duty-free items you may take into Norway and, when returning home, into your own country (the age limit for import of alcoholic beverages is 20, for tobacco products 16):

Into:	Cigarettes		Cigars		Tobacco	Spirits		Wine
Norway*	200		250 g.		250 g.	1 l.	and	1 l.
		or		or			or	
	(400)		(500 g.)		(500 g.)	1 l.	or	2 l.
Australia	250	or	250 g.	or	250 g.	1 l.	or	1 l.
Canada	200	and	50	and	900 g.	1.1 l.	or	1.1 l.
Eire	200	or	50	or	250g.	1 l.	and	2 l.
N.Zealand	200	or	50	or	250 g.	1.1 l.	and	4.5 l.
S.Africa	400	and	50	and	250 g.	1 l.	and	2 l.
U.K.	200	or	50	or	250 g.	1 l.	and	2 l.
U.S.A.	200	and	100	and	**	1 l.	or	1 l.

* The figures in parentheses are for non-European visitors only
** a reasonable quantity

Spirits containing more than 60% alcohol (120° proof) are prohibited.

Currency restrictions: There is no restriction on the amount of currency you can import. On leaving the country, you may take out local currency up to 5,000 kroner and foreign monies up to the amount imported.

DRIVING IN NORWAY. To take a car into Norway, you'll need:

● a valid driving licence
● car registration papers
● insurance coverage (the most common formula is the Green Card)
● a national identity sticker
● a red warning triangle

D   **Driving regulations**. The use of seat belts is obligatory, and that includes back-seat passengers if the car is so equipped. Motorcycle riders and their passengers must wear crash helmets. Dipped (lowbeam) headlights must be switched on, even in broad daylight. All the basic rules for right-hand traffic apply. More than elsewhere, though, the following rule should be observed: drive slowly. The roads simply do not permit high speeds, and you are unlikely to be able to cover stretches of more than about 400 kilometres a day. In western Norway, where you also have ferries to cope with, you shouldn't even count on driving more than 200 a day.

The sign with an inverted red triangle means yield right-of-way. It is extensively used at spots where other European countries would use a STOP sign; remember, then, that this sign is an imperative order to yield to the traffic ahead.

Farm animals, reindeer and elk frequently cross or meander down country roads. Signs will sometimes warn you of cattle or elk crossings ahead, but stay alert at all times. Animals always have right of way, and farmers are entitled to charge full butcher rates for any animal killed by a car, regardless of the circumstances.

Speed limits. Norway has two basic speed limits: 50 kilometres per hour (32 m.p.h.) in towns and residential areas, 80 k.p.h. (50 m.p.h.) elsewhere, except on *some* stretches of motorway, on which 90 k.p.h. (56 m.p.h.) is permitted. Coaches and buses are never allowed to exceed 80 k.p.h. Other heavy vehicles and cars towing caravans (trailers) are restricted to 70 k.p.h. (60 if the caravan does not have its own independent brakes). Note that in some localities only the sign bearing the place's name indicates that one is entering a residential area.

Distance

Fuel and oil *(bensin; olje)*. Even though Norway produces its own petrol, prices are high. Service stations (with a wide assortment of brands) are plentiful in urban areas, less so in the country. If you're driving through the mountains, don't risk letting your petrol tank get too low; it may be a long way to the next filling station.

112

Fluid measures

imp. gals. 0 ——————————— 5 ——————————— 10

liters 0 5 10 20 30 40 50

U.S. gals. 0 ——————————— 5 ——————————— 10

Parking. Regulations are strict, and violations invariably entail fines, even for foreigners. Meters are found in the centre of major cities. In Oslo, yellow meters indicate a maximum of one hour's parking; grey meters, two hours; brown, maximum three hours. In addition, red meters indicate a maximum of 15 minutes' parking. If you park in a no-stopping area, you risk having your car towed away. Oslo's Traffic Board issues a leaflet called *Parking Regulations*, explaining the complexities of the local regulations; it's available from the Tourist Office.

Drinking and driving. It is forbidden to drive with an alcohol content of more than 0.05% in the blood. The average person would reach this level by drinking a single whisky and soda. If found guilty, the penalty is 21 days in prison, plus confiscation of your driving licence for at least six months. Foreigners benefit from no particular indulgence. There are frequent spot traffic controls in towns and along major roads, and anyone suspected of having consumed alcohol will be put through a test.

Breakdowns. You'll find the dealer of your car make in the classified telephone directory under "Bilverksteder" (garages), or call one of the rescue services:

Oslo	*Falken*	tel. 95 00 00 for immediate aid
		tel. 23 25 85 for ordinary problems
	Viking	tel. 60 60 90
Bergen	*Falken*	tel. 20 13 10
	Viking	tel. 29 22 22

Road signs. International pictographic road signs are used, but the following signs with Norwegian texts are worth memorizing:

All stans forbudt	No stopping
Datoparkering	Night parking at one side of the street only (even numbers on even days, odd numbers on odd days)
Ferist	Cattle grid

D	Grusvei/Løs grus	Gravelled road
	Kjør sakte	Drive slowly
	Møteplass	Passing place on side of the road
	Omkjøring	Deviation (Detour)
	Svake kanter	Soft shoulders
	Teleløsning / Teleløyse	Pot-hole due to frost
	Veiarbeid	Roadworks (Men working)

driving licence	**førerkort/kjørekort/sertifikat**
car registration papers	**vognkort**
Green Card	**grønt kort**
Check the oil/tyres/battery, please.	**Sjekk oljen/dekkene/batteriet, er De snill**.
I've had a breakdown.	**Jeg har fått motorstopp**.
There's been an accident.	**Det har skjedd en ulykke**.

Driving in Oslo and Bergen. Unfortunately, to get into Oslo by car you have to pay—at one of the 18 toll stations that ring the capital, covering all roads in. You can drive across the centre of the city in a couple of minutes—avoiding a lot of traffic—if you take the tunnel that runs beneath the harbour district. Bergen also has toll stations (4). To reach the northern side of Bergen, avoid the centre by taking the tunnel.

Oslo–Bergen route. Two roads connect Oslo and Bergen. The Haukelifjell route, Oslo–Drammen–Kongsberg–Notodden–Røldal–Odda–Kinsarvik–Bergen, is open all year round. The second, and perhaps more scenic, possibility, the Hallingdal route, is partly closed in winter. Heading north-west from Oslo through Hønefoss–Gol–Geilo and Kinsarvik to Bergen, it follows, more or less, the Bergen Railway line (see p. 43) to Haugastøl. There are also three ferry-free routes from east to west.

E **EMBASSIES and CONSULATES**. Embassies and consulates are listed in the classified telephone directory under "Ambassader" and "Konsulater".

Embassies/Consulates in Oslo:

Canada	Oscars gt. 20; tel. 46 69 55
United Kingdom	Thomas Heftyes gt. 8; tel. 55 24 00
U.S.A.	Drammensveien 18; tel. 44 85 50

Consulate in Bergen:

United Kingdom	Carl Konows gt. 34; tel. (05) 34 85 05

EMERGENCIES. See also MEDICAL CARE. In case of accident or other emergencies, phone (in Oslo and Bergen):

Ambulance	003
Fire	001
Police	002

GUIDES. On tours and at major tourist attractions, there's every likelihood you'll have English-, German- and French-speaking guides. The services of a licensed guide can be secured in Oslo through the Guide-Service at the Tourist Information Office (tel. 83 83 80), and in Bergen through the Tourist Information Office or the Bergen Guide Service, Slottsgt. 1 (tel. 32 77 00).

HAIRDRESSERS* *(frisør)*. Most big hotels have their own salons. Women's hairdressers are listed in the classified section of the telephone directory under "Damefrisører", barbers under "Herrefrisører", beauty salons under "Hudpleie". Rates vary somewhat from one establishment to another and are never low. Tipping is not customary.

haircut	**klipp**
shampoo and set	**vask og legg**
shampoo and blow-dry	**vask og føning**
permanent wave	**permanent**

HITCH-HIKING *(haiking)*. Hitch-hiking is not easy, and is banned on motorways. Vehicles on the road in summer tend to be crowded and fully packed, leaving little room for any additional passengers, and when drivers do stop, it's at their own risk and they are responsible for a passenger's safety.

Can you give me/us a lift to …?	**Kan jeg/vi få sitte på til …?**

LANGUAGE. Language in Norway is not as thorny a problem as in some parts of the world, but it is complex. Here's what happened historically.

First there was *riksmål*, the only official language, which evolved during hundreds of years of Danish domination. But while preachers and teachers went by the *riksmål* book, people in all the regions were speaking their own dialects. In the middle of the 19th century a new language, *landsmål*, was created. It was a Norwegian Esperanto, an artificial concoction of bits and pieces from various

L dialects. Since then, both languages have evolved and, to add extra confusion to outsiders, their names have been changed. *Riksmål* is now called *bokmål* ("book language") and *landsmål* is *nynorsk* ("new Norwegian"). Luckily, the languages are similar enough for Norwegians to be able to talk to each other.

Luckily for foreigners, too, in the cities you can virtually count on everybody having at the very least a modicum of English; outside in the country, however, you may well meet situations where the odd phrase in Norwegian will help you (see p. 126).

There are 29 letters in the Norwegian alphabet: the 26 "English" letters followed by "æ" (usually pronounced like **a** in b**a**d), "ø" (pronounced like **ir** in b**ir**d) and "å" (like **aw** in s**aw**). Note this when you look in a telephone directory.

The Berlitz phrase book, NORWEGIAN FOR TRAVELLERS, covers practically all situations you're likely to encounter in your travels in Norway, and the Norwegian-English/English-Norwegian pocket dictionary contains some 12,500 concepts, plus a special menu-reader supplement.

Good morning	**God morgen**
Good afternoon	**God dag**
Good evening	**God aften/kveld**
Good night	**God natt**
Hello/Hi	**Hallo/Hei**
Good-bye	**Adjø**
Bye!	**Ha det!**

LAUNDRY and DRY-CLEANING. Major hotels offer same-day service on weekdays. If laundry services are unavailable, the hotel receptionist will direct you to a nearby establishment, or you can look for addresses in the classified section of the telephone directory under "Vaskerier og strykerier". Unfortunately, laundry and dry-cleaning are expensive, and self-service laundromats are not very common.

LOST PROPERTY (*hittegods*). In Oslo, the general lost property office is at:

Grønlandsleiret 44; tel. 66 98 65 (open during normal office hours)
For trolleys/trams: Nationaltheatret Stasjon; tel. 66 49 27
For trains: Central Railway Station; tel. 36 80 47

In Bergen, enquire at the police station at Rådstuplass 8; tel. 21 65 20.

MAPS. Simplified city maps are generally included in the range of free-of-charge tourist brochures to be found at airports, hotels, travel agencies and tourist offices. Book stores and kiosks will have a good assortment of reasonably priced maps. A fine tourist map of the entire country, *Norway by Car*, published by the Norway Travel Association, is available free of charge at most travel agencies and tourist information offices.

The maps in this book were prepared by Falk-Verlag, Hamburg, who also publish a large-scale map of Oslo.

a street plan of …   **et kart over …**
a road map of this region   **et veikart over dette området**

MEDICAL CARE. Through a British-Norwegian health agreement, no charge is made for Britons staying in Norwegian hospitals, and outpatients will have part of their doctor's fees refunded. For nationals of other countries, it is sensible to take out health insurance covering the risk of illness or accident while on holiday. An insurance representative or travel agent at home will be able to advise.

Most hotels maintain contact with a doctor who can be summoned at short notice. (Doctors are listed in the classified section of the telephone directory under "Leger".)

Oslo has three clinics for **medical emergencies** *(legevakt)*. One is open day and night, all year round:

Oslo Municipal Policlinic, Storgt. 40; tel. 11 70 70

Bergen Municipal Policlinic, Lars Hillesgt. 30; tel. 32 11 20 (day and night).

Dental emergencies *(tannlegevakt)*:
Oslo, Kolstadgt. 18; tel. 67 48 46 (8–11 p.m. daily; Saturdays, Sundays and holidays also 11 a.m.–2 p.m.)

Bergen, Lars Hillesgt. 30; tel. 32 11 20 (10–11 a.m. and 6.30–9 p.m. daily)

Chemists or drugstores *(apotek)* don't stock the wide range of goods that you find in the equivalent shop in Britain or the U.S. For perfume, cosmetics, etc., you must go to a *parfymeri*. All-night pharmacies:

Oslo, Jernbanetorvets apotek, Jernbanetorget 4B (Central Railway Station); tel. 41 24 82

Bergen, Apoteket Nordstjernen, Busterminal (Strømsgt. 8); tel. 31 68 84   **117**

M **MEETING PEOPLE.** Outsiders have a habit of lumping all Scandinavians together, a habit that is not greatly appreciated by the countries concerned. If one were to generalize, it is usually said that the Danes are the most approachable of the Northern peoples, the Swedes the most formal and the Norwegians lie somewhere between the two: more contemplative and more reticent than the former, less severe and inflexible than the latter. *If* one were to generalize.

Norwegians are intensely proud of their country and its nature, but have no illusions about its size or role in the world. You may be surprised at how conscious they are of the state of affairs and activities of other countries. Norwegians do not generally make a fuss of visitors, nor are they likely to open a conversation with strangers; you will normally have to make the first move. But once you have made the initial effort, you'll be assured of a warm welcome wherever you go.

MONEY MATTERS

Currency. The Norwegian unit of currency is the *krone* ("crown"), generally abbreviated kr. It is divided into 100 *øre*.

Coins: 10 and 50 øre; kr 1, 5 and 10.

Banknotes: kr 50, 100, 500 and 1,000.

For currency restrictions, see CUSTOMS AND ENTRY REGULATIONS.

Banks and currency exchange. Banks are open from 8.15 a.m. to 3.30 p.m., Monday to Wednesday and on Fridays, until 5 or 6 p.m. on Thursdays. In the period between June 1 and August 31, however, they close at 3 p.m. (5 or 5.30 p.m. on Thursdays).

Oslo Airport: 7 a.m.–10 p.m. daily, 7 a.m.–7 p.m. Saturday; Oslo Central Railway Station: 8 a.m.–7.30 p.m., Monday–Saturday, 12 noon–6 p.m. Sunday (in summer 7 a.m.–11 p.m. daily).

Most large hotels will change foreign currency, but at less favourable rates.

Credit cards and traveller's cheques. Major international credit cards (*kredittkort*) will be honoured in most large hotels and restaurants and in many department stores and tourist shops. Traveller's cheques (*reisesjekk*) are easy to cash almost everywhere provided you have proper identification.

Sales tax. Called *moms*, the value-added tax on purchased items (10–14%) can be refunded for foreign visitors. For details, see Shopping, page 90.

NEWSPAPERS and MAGAZINES *(avis; blad)*. You will find an excellent assortment of foreign-language newspapers and magazines at most centrally located kiosks, as well as at most large hotels, airports and railway and bus stations.

OSLO CARD. The Oslo Card, or *Oslo-kortet*, offers visitors the chance to see the city at a fair price. Similar in appearance to a credit card, it allows the holder free entry to museums and sights, free public transport, reductions on car hire, sightseeing tours and hotel rates. Used to the full, it represents a considerable bargain. The pass is valid for one, two or three days and is available at hotels, stores and the Tourist Office.

PETS. Owing to the risk of rabies, very stringent rules, including lengthy quarantine, are in force for the import of dogs, cats and other animals into Norway. A prior permit *must* be obtained from the Norwegian Ministry of Agriculture. The smuggling of pets into Norway is subject to heavy fines and perhaps the loss of the pet.

PHOTOGRAPHY. All major brands of film are available. Restrictions on photography, if any, will vary from one institution or museum to another. It is best to enquire in each case.

POLICE. Policemen in strict black uniforms with black kepis patrol on foot, in white cars marked POLITI or on motorcycles. Notably helpful and courteous in the normal course of events, they're absolutely inflexible when it comes to driving offences: for speeding, you'll get a heavy fine, for driving under the influence of alcohol, it's prison.

Police emergency numbers (Oslo and Bergen): 002

Police stations are listed in the telephone directory under "Politiet".

P **PUBLIC HOLIDAYS** *(offentlig høytidsdag/helligdag).* Early closing is on Christmas Eve and New Year's Eve, as well as on Saturday afternoons.

January 1	*Første nyttårsdag*	New Year's Day
May 1	*Arbeidets dag*	Labour Day
May 17	*Grunnlovsdag*	Constitution Day
December 25/26	*Jul*	Christmas
Movable dates:	*Skjærtorsdag*	Maundy Thursday
	Langfredag	Good Friday
	Annen påskedag	Easter Monday
	Kristi himmelfartsdag	Ascension Day
	Annen pinsedag	Whit Monday

Are you open tomorrow?   **Holder De åpent i morgen?**

R **RADIO and TV** *(radio; fjernsyn).* Norsk rikskringkasting, or NRK, the Norwegian Broadcasting Corporation, is state-owned and operates both the radio and television services. Main TV transmission is in the evening. TV films are shown in the original language.

BBC, Voice of America and most European radio stations can easily be received day and night on short wave.

RELIGIOUS SERVICES *(gudstjeneste/messe).* Norway has a Lutheran State Church, to which just about the whole population belongs. However, many other religions are represented. Services and religious meetings are announced in most daily papers.

S **SHOPPING HOURS.** Hours vary enormously. In Oslo, shops normally open from 9 or 10 a.m. to 5 or 7 p.m., Monday to Friday, until 1, 2 or 3 p.m. on Saturdays; closed on Sundays and public holidays. Centrally situated kiosks selling newspapers, tobacco, fruit, sweets, and so on, may stay open till 11 p.m. Kiosks at camping sites are always open till 11 p.m.

Oslo's two large fruit, vegetable and flower markets are open from 7 a.m. to 2 p.m., Monday to Saturday. From mid-March to mid-October: 7 a.m. to 3 p.m. weekdays and till 2 p.m. on Saturdays.

Bergen's picturesque Fish Market is open from Monday to Saturday between 8 a.m. and 3 p.m.

SIGHTSEEING TOURS. In **Oslo**, a typical sample of sightseeing tours, with guide, might include:

- Oslo from the Fjord. 50 minutes. By boat. View of harbour and city, fortress of Akershus and delightful islands of the fjord.
- Fjord Cruise. 2 hours. By boat. On some cruises, lunch or dinner at a reputable restaurant ashore is included. Other operators offer "picnic" cruises.
- City Tour. 3 hours, morning or afternoon. By coach. Variously includes visits to City Hall, Vigeland Sculpture Park, Holmenkollen Ski Jump, Akershus Castle, Edvard Munch Museum, Viking Ships and Kon-Tiki Museum.
- City Tour. All day, with lunch. By coach and boat. Includes visits to Polar Ship Fram, Kon-Tiki Raft, Norwegian Folk Museum, Viking Ships, Vigeland Sculpture Park and Holmenkollen Ski Jump, plus fjord cruise.

In **Bergen**, these are the most usual tours offered:

- City Tour, with excursion to Troldhaugen. 3 hours. By coach. Includes visits to Old Bergen Museum and Troldhaugen, home of the composer Grieg.
- City Tour. 2 hours, afternoon. By coach. Old and new Bergen, with visits to the Assembly Rooms and Fantoft Stave Church.
- City Tour. 1 ½ hours, early evening. By coach. General view of Bergen.
- Excursion to Hardangerfjord. All day, with stop for lunch. By coach, train. Tour of area surrounding one of Norway's most romantic fjords.
- Norway in a Nutshell (see p. 60). All day, with stop for lunch in Flåm. By train, bus and boat. Tour covering Norway's most spectacular scenery, fjords and mountains, lakes and forests.
- Minicruise to Sognefjord and Nordfjord. 2 days. By boat. Price including full pension.

Most fjord cruises or coach/fjord cruises operate in the summer season only. Tourist offices supply detailed information of specific tour operators and tours.

TIME DIFFERENCES. Norway follows Central European Time, GMT + 1. In summer, the clock is put one hour ahead (GMT + 2):

T

New York	London	**Norway**	Jo'burg	Sydney	Auckland
6 a.m.	11 a.m.	**noon**	noon	8 p.m.	10 p.m.

What time is it, please?   **Hvor mange er klokken?**

TIPPING. The service charge is included in hotel bills, but porters should be tipped individually. It is also included in restaurant bills, although a little extra is frequently added if you are satisfied with the meal and the service. Some further indications:

Hotel porter, per bag	kr 5
Maid, for extra services	kr 10
Waiter	5–10% (optional)
Lavatory attendant	charges posted or kr 3
Taxi driver	10% (optional)
Tour guide	optional

TOILETS. Public facilities are located at stations, in department stores and in some of the squares and parks, and are generally designated pictographically, but may also be marked "Toaletter", "WC", "Damer"/"Herrer" or "D"/"H".

TOURIST INFORMATION OFFICES (*turistinformasjon*). Norwegian tourist offices abroad will help you to plan your holiday before you leave home:

United Kingdom   Norwegian Tourist Board, Charles House
5–11,Lower Regent St., London SW1Y 4LR;
tel. (071) 839 26 50

U.S.A.   Scandinavian National Tourist Offices,
655 Third Avenue, 18th floor, New York, NY 10017;
tel. (212) 949-2333

In Norway, contact NORTRA:

Langkaia 1, 0150 N-Oslo 1; tel. (02) 42 70 44

The Oslo Tourist Board—Oslo Reiselivsråd—has its head office at the following address:

Rådhusgt. 19, 0158 Oslo 1; tel. (02) 42 71 70

Its Tourist Information Office in the City Hall (enter from the harbour side) also provides advice, brochures and maps, and publishes an excellent free *Oslo Guide*, available in several languages, as well as a pamphlet, *What's on in Oslo*.

The Bergen Tourist Board—Bergen Reiselivslag:

Slottsgt. 1, N-5000 Bergen; tel. (05) 31 38 60

Tourist Information Office:

Torgalmenningen; tel. (05) 32 14 80

This office also issues a *Bergen Guide*. Local tourist offices throughout the country are indicated by the international sign, a white **i** on a green background.

TRANSPORT*. See also CAR HIRE.

To get around **Oslo**, you have a choice between buses *(buss)*, trams/street-cars *(trikk)* and underground railways *(undergrunnsbane/T-bane)*—which emerge into daylight on the suburban network. The terminal for all underground lines is Stortinget Stasjon, in Karl Johans Gate, at Egertoget.

The bus terminal for suburban buses is at Gallery Oslo (Shweigaardsgt. 8–10, next to the Central Railway Station), but most buses run through the centre of town, stopping at Wessels Plass next to the Parliament Building and by the National Theatre.

Single tickets (valid for transfers within one hour) are available from the driver and at stations, as are multi-journey cards of 5 (*Minikort*) or 12 (*Maxikort*) coupons which allow unlimited transfer within one hour from the time they are stamped. A 24-hour tourist ticket can be obtained at the Tourist Information Office, City Hall. Information about timetables and fares can be had at Trafikanten, Jernbanetorget, tel. 17 70 30.

Bergen is served by buses and trolley buses offering a special tourist ticket valid for 48 hours, available at the Tourist Information Office. and at most hotels. Buses for Bergen's suburbs leave from the Central Bus Station at Strømsgt. 8, the same terminal as for the airport bus.

T   **Taxi** *(drosje/taxi)*. All taxis are metered. Ranks are scattered throughout Oslo and Bergen; see the telephone directory under "Drosjer" for the nearest one. Taxi drivers rarely cruise for passengers and are not allowed to pick up customers within 100 metres of a taxi rank. (Customers waiting at the rank have priority.) When cars are free, the TAXI sign on the roof is lit.

Train *(tog)*. The Norwegian State Railways—Norges Statsbaner, or NSB—operate a punctual network, with Oslo Central Railway Station *(Oslo Sentralstasjon)* as its main terminal. There are connections to Sweden and to the continent via Copenhagen, the main inland destinations being Stavanger, Bergen and Trondheim, with connections to Bodø, Norway's northernmost railway station (from Narvik, there are connections to Sweden only).

Some long-distance trains have carriages especially equipped for parents with babies and for people in wheelchairs. Seat reservations should be made, especially on express trains *(ekspresstog)*, such as the Oslo–Bergen Railway *(Bergensbanen)*. Children under four years old travel free. Users under 16 and old-age pensioners pay half-price.

Enquire at any travel agency or railway station about special group, family and weekday tickets. *Eurailpasses* and *Inter-Rail tickets* are valid in Norway; furthermore the *Nordic Tourist Ticket (Nordturist)* permits 21 days of unlimited rail travel in Denmark, Finland, Norway and Sweden.

Car ferry *(bilferge/-ferje)*. Travelling on roads in western Norway involves numerous fjord crossings by ferry boat—there's usually no other way to go. The frequency of ferry services depends on the season. In rural areas, local hotels will always be able to tell you exact ferry times, but the Norway Travel Association regularly prints a reliable schedule, *Tourist Timetables*, which can be picked up at most tourist offices. Fares vary according to size and weight of vehicles.

single (one-way) ticket	**enkeltbillett**
return (round-trip) ticket	**tur-returbillett**
first/second class	**første/annen klasse**

DAYS OF THE WEEK

Monday	**mandag**	Friday	**fredag**
Tuesday	**tirsdag**	Saturday	**lørdag**
Wednesday	**onsdag**	Sunday	**søndag**
Thursday	**torsdag**		

MONTHS

January	**januar**	July	**juli**
February	**februar**	August	**august**
March	**mars**	September	**september**
April	**april**	October	**oktober**
May	**mai**	November	**november**
June	**juni**	December	**desember**

NUMBERS

0	**null**	21	**tjueen**
1	**en**	22	**tjueto**
2	**to**	30	**tretti**
3	**tre**	31	**trettien**
4	**fire**	32	**trettito**
5	**fem**	40	**førti**
6	**seks**	50	**femti**
7	**syv/sju**	60	**seksti**
8	**åtte**	70	**sytti**
9	**ni**	80	**åtti**
10	**ti**	90	**nitti**
11	**elleve**	100	**hundre**
12	**tolv**	101	**hundreogen**
13	**tretten**	121	**hundreogtjueen**
14	**fjorten**	200	**to hundre**
15	**femten**	300	**tre hundre**
16	**seksten**	1,000	**tusen**
17	**sytten**	1,100	**et tusen et hundre**
18	**atten**	2,000	**to tusen**
19	**nitten**	50,000	**femti tusen**
20	**tjue**	100,000	**hundre tusen**

SOME USEFUL EXPRESSIONS

yes/no	**ja/nei**
please/thank you	**vær så snill/takk**
excuse me	**unnskyld**
where/when/how	**hvor/når/hvordan**
how long/how far	**hvor lenge/hvor langt**
yesterday/today/tomorrow	**i går/i dag/i morgen**
day/week/month/year	**dag/uke/måned/år**
left/right	**venstre/høyre**
big/small	**stor/liten**
cheap/expensive	**billig/dyr**
hot/cold	**varm/kald**
open/closed	**åpen/lukket**
free (vacant)/occupied	**ledig/opptatt**

Does anyone here speak English? **Er det noen her som snakker engelsk?**

What does this mean? **Hva betyr dette?**

I don't understand. **Jeg forstår ikke.**

Please write it down. **Kan De skrive det?**

Waiter!/Waitress! **Kelner!/Frøken!**

I'd like … **Jeg vil gjerne ha …**

How much is that? **Hvor mye koster det?**

Just a minute. **Et øyeblikk.**

Where are the toilets? **Hvor er toalettet?**

126 Could you help me, please? **Kan De hjelpe meg?**

Index

An asterisk (*) next to a page number indicates a map reference.